The VERSIFICATION *of*
ROBERT BROWNING

The VERSIFICATION *of* ROBERT BROWNING

BY

HARLAN HENTHORNE HATCHER

Phaeton Press

New York

1968

Originally Published 1928

Reprinted 1969

Published by Phaeton Press, Inc.

Library of Congress Catalog Card Number 73-90360

TO

D. H.

FOR HER SENSITIVE EAR
AND PATIENT HEART

PREFACE

THIS STUDY was undertaken at the suggestion of Dr. C. E. Andrews, who is able to make prosody seem important to human happiness. The general point of view from which it is written, and many of the problems with which it deals, were worked out in his seminars in *Poetic Rhythm*. The study has had the advantage of his constant interest and criticism, which, like rivulets, have swelled the main current of the stream. Professor M. O. Percival has been liberal with his time and has made valuable suggestions. It is a pleasure to thank, also, Professors J. V. Denney, J. R. Taylor, G. H. McKnight, and Hans Kurath for their careful reading of the manuscript, and for their helpful criticisms. Professor W. L. Graves very kindly read the early chapters, and Dr. M. B. Ogle the chapter on classical rhythms.

H. H. H.

Columbus, Ohio,

CONTENTS

PART ONE

CHAPTER I

INTRODUCTION

THIS STUDY has attempted to show, by a minute examination of his poems, upon what metrical principles Browning worked and what his actual practice was. He never expressed himself about theory except in the most general terms, and what he did say concerned the subject matter of poetry rather than its form. He quoted doggerel to people who came to the Casa Guidi expecting to hear him talk about and recite his verse. He did on occasion make light of poetic form for its own sake; he called versification the "mere outward crust" of the thought, and he spoke of the final moulding of a poem as "hitching it into verse." This attitude must have been something of a pose, however. He studiously avoided mere prettiness and consciously strewed nettles and burs as well as cowslips through his poetic meadows. He thought poetry should be solid and manly, not a "substitute for a cigar or a game of dominoes to an idle man." All that he said about versification could be summed up in the words of Richard Rolle of Hampole,

> For I rek noght, thogh the ryme be rude,
> If the maters thar-of be gude.

or in his own words from the *Inn Album,*

> That bard's a Browning; he neglects the form:
> But, ah, the sense, ye Gods, the weighty sense! (1.17-18)

In fact, the principles of his art, like those of Shakespeare, are never consciously set forth by the poet himself; they must be discovered by a careful study of the finished works.

3

Everybody has impressions of Browning's versification, that it is rough and harsh, or smooth and melodious, or something between the two; but no one has undertaken to find out exactly what rules of verse or system of prosody Browning practiced. Professor Saintsbury writes pleasantly about Browning in those important personal essays which comprise his *History of English Prosody*, but the charmed (or impatient) reader finds little to carry away with him; and a closer examination of Browning's poems than Professor Saintsbury was able to make sometimes leads one into disagreement with his broad but confident generalizations, as when he says, "As a matter of fact Browning, though an audacious, is almost invariably a correct prosodist—he goes often to the very edge, but hardly ever over it." If being a correct prosodist means, as we believe, never straining the metrical pattern beyond the power of the reader to preserve it, even the qualifying "almost invariably" and "hardly" are not enough to preserve the generalization. But of this the reader may judge when he has examined the following chapters.

Whatever value the work may have is independent of any one metrical theory. Everybody will agree in general upon the validity and observability of the phenomona in Browning's verse; many will disagree with any system of prosody employed to describe them. One must face this unfortunate situation, however, and beg that the attention of the reader be centered upon the phenomena rather than the method of describing them. Some principle had of necessity to be adopted to present the material at all, and we have of course stated it in terms which seem to us best to describe the principles of our verse.

We have proceeded therefore on the theory that the

fundamental characteristic of verse, which distinguishes it from prose, is that verse is regularly divided into measures of approximately equal time intervals by a succession of blows, or accents. These measures, or time parts, by their regular recurrence, give the ear the sense of rhythm. In this respect at least verse and music are analogous.

The analogy could be pressed much farther if it were advantageous to do so; but strict musical terms are better suited to a general description of the fundamental nature of verse than of the details of a poet's versification. The temporal equality of the measures is taken for granted throughout the study, and time-signature is omitted, except for dipodic or quadruple measures in four-four time. But the distinctive effects of different lines are achieved not by the temporal equality of the measures, but by their syllabic structure. To say that ordinary (that is, not-dipodic) verse is in three-eight or three-four time does not distinguish such different lines as,

Like the skipping of rabbits by moonlight,—three slim shapes,

and

What, there's nothing in the moon noteworthy?

In the study of a poet's technique, therefore, detailed consideration must be given to the variation in the syllabic pattern of the lines; and the principles of his versification can best be stated in terms of the syllabic structure of the measures. It makes considerable difference whether the time of a measure is filled up by one, two, three, or four syllables.

We have adopted the musical analogy by placing the bar before the syllable which carries the accent, since a measure cannot be felt to begin until the blow has set up a point in time from which to measure. This division into measures sets up for each type of verse a metrical pattern as its structural basis. For blank verse it is one of five measures of two syllables each, with the accent falling on the even ones. This pattern is immediately established in the mind of the reader, and in its ideal form it seldom exists elsewhere. But it sets up within him the anticipation of its recurrence, and his ear is always reaching forward, as it were, to find its expectancy fulfilled in the words of the poem.

But words arranged into phrases do not fit into a continuously regular pattern; for we do not talk in iambs or anapests. They occupy a little more or a little less time than the reader expected, or the natural speech rhythms resist the restraint or the confines of the imposed metrical pattern. The reader is then called upon to assimilate into the expected pattern some unexpected elements, and this always introduces an element of surprise. But it is precisely this subtle conflict between the expected and the unexpected that prevents monotony in good verse. The poets have been careful to introduce certain departures from the anticipated pattern to tease the ear away from the boredom of finding only what it expects. So long as these departures are not too far removed from the usual, the ear is pleased and the versification is called good. If they depart too far, or introduce conflicts which too stubbornly resist order or cannot be assimilated into the pattern at all, the expected pattern collapses on the reader or the rhythm of the new phrases sets up a new pattern of its own. This phenomenon occurs often in Browning. He introduces lines which resist coercion and ride lordly over the pattern of their neighbors with a rhythm of their own.

The study of a poet's versification therefore consists in describing the patterns which different poems set up in the mind of the reader, and in noting the types of departures and their frequency which the poet introduces and asks the reader to accept and assimilate into this pattern. If he is a conservative poet, like Milton, he will not depart very far from the expected pattern; but if he is unconventional, individual, and aggressive, he will call upon all the powers of his reader, perhaps indeed make demands which he cannot meet. If Browning could dance on the very edge, many of his readers have grown dizzy and fallen over. He was able to incorporate into his patterns elements which less aggressive readers could not subdue.

No one will be greatly surprised that the study terminates in rules less formal and precise than those which Mr. Bridges was able to construct for Milton. For Browning took the greatest freedom in his versification and seemed conscious of no very definite rules of any kind. But what he was trying to do, and what he did do, we have attempted to set down in some detail in the ensuing chapters.

CHAPTER II

HABITS OF COMPOSITION
AND REVISION

ROSSETTI SAID that Marston said that "Browning's system of composition is to write down on a slate, in prose, what he wants to say, and then turn it into verse, striving after the greatest amount of condensation possible; thus, if an exclamation will suggest his meaning, he substitutes this for a whole sentence." [1] Undoubtedly this is another of the pleasant apocryphal stories about Browning, but it illustrates a notion still current as to his method of composition.

He did compose with great rapidity, two steps at a time, as if he were rushing up the steps of the Casa Guidi. His poetry shows the same boundless energy that his personality reflected. Like most other poets, he first worked out his poems in his head before he attempted composition. Sometimes the plan of his work came upon him immediately. He found the Old Yellow Book in June, 1859, and mastered the contents on his way home. It immediately laid powerful hold on his imagination. Lehmann may have antedated the following incident (as Dowden suggests), but it could easily be accurate. " 'When I had read the book,' so Browning told me, 'my plan was at once settled. I went for a walk, gathered twelve pebbles from the road, and put them at equal distances on the parapet that bordered it. Those represented the twelve chapters into which the poem is divided, and I adhered to

[1] *The Preraphaelite Brotherhood Journal*, Feb. 28, 1850. Quoted, Dowden: *Life of Robert Browning*, p. 36 (Everyman's ed.).

that arrangement to the last,' " [2]   The amazing achievement of this poem is an example of Browning's energy and industry.

There are conflicting statements about the time of composition of *The Ring and the Book*, but apparently it was written in about four years.[3] In 1862 Browning says the poem is fully conceived in his mind, but is still unwritten. He began the actual composition in October, 1864, after the publication of *Dramatis Personae* was out of his way. The story of its progress as told by Browning himself is recorded by Rossetti in his diary for March 15, 1868. Browning had called that Sunday. "He began it (*The Ring and the Book*) in October '64. . . He says he writes day by day on a regular systematic plan—some three hours in the early part of the day; he seldom or never, unless in quite brief poems, feels the inspiring impulse and sets the thing down into words at the same time—often stores up a subject long before he writes it. He has written his forthcoming work all consecutively—not some of the later parts before the earlier."[4]

The work was nearly complete at the time this was written, but Browning was willing to delay its publication nearly eight months if necessary to its perfection.. It began to appear in November, 1868, just four years after its beginning. The actual composition had consumed a little more than three years, and the completed poem contained 20,988 lines, almost exactly twice as many as *Paradise Lost* with 10,565. It is interesting to recall that Milton had made a tentative beginning on his great epic in 1642, began composi-

[2]R. Lehmann: *An Artist's Reminiscences*, p. 224. Quoted, Dowden: *op. cit.* p. 253.

[3] I can find no evidence for the statement of Morton and others that the work was composed in two years.

[4] W. M. Rossetti: *Rossetti Papers*, 1862-1870, p. 302.

tion on the present form of the poem in 1657-8, and published it in 1666 after nearly nine years of labor. At the same rate, Milton would have required eighteen years to write *The Ring and the Book,* while Browning would have tossed off *Paradise Lost* in a mere eighteen months.[5]

Browning both planned and wrote *Paracelsus* in about a year. It is nearly half as long as *Paradise Lost* (4,152 lines). Tennyson required three years to write *The Princess,* which is almost a thousand lines shorter than *Paracelsus.*[6] If Browning is correct in his dates in the letter to Milsand,[7] *Sordello* was written in 1838, a little more than two years after *Paracelsus.* It is a long and difficult composition. According to Rossetti's story which he had from Browning's father, he could write a drama with unbelievable haste. "Once when the poet was kept indoors a few days by illness, his father, who was living in another house, on going to visit him was each day received boisterously and cheerfully with the words: 'I've done another act, father.' He was writing *The Blot on the Scutcheon,* and he finished it in five days."[8] In his later life especially he usually finished a work on the day set. The story of the *Inn Album* was decided upon and constructed in a single morning, to be carried out precisely as planned. He considered twenty or thirty lines a day a good rate of production, and his manuscript showed few corrections.[9] *Luria* was one of the very few of his poems which caused him any continued travail.[10] He

[5] Milton's handicap must qualify these comparisons, but even so they are extremely interesting.

[6] Published Dec. 25, 1847. He had 200 lines in a "butcher's book" May, 1845. (Lounsbury: *Life and Times of Tennyson,* p. 531.)

[7] Preface to *Sordello.* 1863.

[8] *Letters of Dante G. Rossetti to Wm. Allingham,* 1854-1870, p. 168.

[9] Cary: *Browning: Poet and Man,* pp. 204-5.

[10] See repeated references in the Browning Letters.

apparently never spent a whole week trying to find the right word, as Wordsworth was said to have done, and Thomas Moore. Indeed, one must go back to the versatile Elizabethans for a parallel to Browning's rapid creation.

His general habits of composition were much like those of other poets, allowing of course for individual eccentricities. Coleridge composed while walking over uneven ground, or breaking through struggling branches of copsewood.[11] *The Ancient Mariner* was worked out on a walk over the Quantock Hills. Wordsworth always wrote, when he could, walking up and down a straight gravel walk, or in some spot where the continuity of his verse met with no collateral interruption.[12] Scott composed much on horseback. Tennyson composed his verse in his garden, or in his private tower, under clouds of smoke from his pipe. There are few such anecdotes about Browning. Sharp, in his *Life of Browning,* said that the inspiration for *Paracelsus* came from midnight walks in Dulwich woods, and that the poem was composed in part in the open air with the glow of distant London with its multitudes as the emotional background. *As I Ride* was composed on horseback during a time when Browning was riding daily for his health.[13]

The habit of systematic daily composition which Rossetti speaks of was certainly not developed until late in life. The *Letters* show him following mood rather than the clock. One can imagine *The Ring and the Book* being composed three hours a day on schedule; but not the *Dramatic Lyrics.* The method of working out the plan of the poem before advancing to composi-

[11] Hazlitt: *My First Acquaintance With Poets.*
[12] Hazlitt: *My First Acquaintance With Poets.*
[13] Domett: "Diary 1873." *Living Age,* 244:400.

tion was probably his life-long habit. He left no unfinished *Christabels;* nor would an interruption by "some person from Porlock" have beheaded any of his *Kubla Khans.*[14]

Browning probably revised as little as any poet that ever lived. He had a vigorous way of writing finis at the end of his poems; for they were Minerva born. He gave them into the keeping of Levana while he went on to the next thing. It is said that he often did not recognize his own poetic offspring when they were later presented to him in social gatherings, and that he sometimes inquired of their paternity. He possessed no complete edition of his own works until the Browning Society gave him one.[15] If Tennyson criticized Browning for his volume,[16] Browning was outraged by Tennyson's acute sensitiveness to criticism and his mania for revision. He wrote to Miss Barrett, "For Keats and Tennyson to 'go softly all their days' for a gruff word or two is quite inexplicable to me, and always has been. Tennyson reads the *Quarterly* and does as they bid him, with the most solemn face in the world—out goes this, in goes that, all is changed and ranged. Oh me!"[17] And when Tennyson made the drastic revisions in the 1842 edition of his poems, Browning wrote to Alfred Domett a letter of deep concern for what he considered a ruthless tampering with his previous work.[18] He could never have any understanding of a Burton forever re-

[14] W. Hall-Griffin said that the unexpected arrival of Capt. Loyd at Hatcham one morning broke in upon the first inspiration for the *Flight of the Duchess,* and changed the whole course of that poem. *Living Age,* 244:404.

[15] Cary: p. 97.

[16] James Knowles' articles on Tennyson in the *Nineteenth Century,* January, 1893. He writes that Tennyson told Browning that "if he got rid of two-thirds, the remaining third would be finer." Tennyson thought limit imperative, and that if he were to make any mark at all, it must be by shortness; for his predecessors were all diffuse.

[17] *Browning Letters,* Vol. I, p. 19. [18] Lounsbury's *Tennyson,* pp. 399-400.

writing the same book, or a Thomson continually revising *The Seasons.*

These criticisms of each other's poetry grew out of their different poetic creeds which were exactly opposed. Browning was never concerned with mere prettiness; he did not object to a few nettles in his poetic meadows; he was not at all troubled by a few geese in his boat. These things gave his popular contemporary the gravest concern.

After publication, Browning confined his revision almost entirely to correcting printer's errors. Even his youthful *Pauline,* whose paternity he would gladly have denied, was not rewritten when he reluctantly reprinted it in the 1868 edition of his poetry to prevent anyone else from printing it.[19] Many another poet would, like Jeremiah with his early sermons, have revised them into contemporary respectability. But Rosetti records in the Diary for February 13, 1868, after a call from Browning, that *Pauline* is being "republished with proper press corrections—not any rewriting, which he objects to." [20]   We have already

[19] Rossetti had discovered it in the British Museum, suspected its authorship, and copied it out in full. Browning thought it was dead and forgotten, and he was glad of it. When Miss Barrett plead in vain for a copy of the poem (for Browning declared to her that it had nothing to recommend it to anybody, and that it was not even a good example of youthful precocity), she threatened to send immediately to the bookseller for a copy. With characteristic determination she said, "I shall have *Pauline* in a day or two— yes, I shall and must, and WILL." Browning wrote back, "Will you, and must you have *Pauline?* If I could pray you to revoke that decision! For it is altogether foolish and *not boylike*—and I shall, I confess, hate the notion of running over it—yet commented it must be; more than mere correction! I was unluckily *precocious*—but I had rather you SAW real infantine efforts (verses at six years old, and drawings still earlier) than this ambiguous, feverish—Why not wait? When you speak of the 'Bookseller'—I smile, in glorious security—having a whole bale of sheets at the house-top. He never knew my name even! and I withdrew these after a very little time." (*Letters,* Vol. I, p. 400.) Miss Barrett did not see *Pauline* just then.

[20] *Rossetti Papers,* p. 299. He had written to Miss Barrett back in January 12, 1846, "Must you see *Pauline?* At least then let me wait a few days; to correct the misprints which affect the sense, and to write you the history of it; what is necessary you should know before you see it." (*Letters,* p. 390.)

seen his attitude toward Tennyson's rewriting of his poems.

It would be an error, however, to suppose from these expressed aversions that Browning never did revise or rewrite his poetry. The 1849 edition of the Poems contained this preface: "Many of these pieces were out of print, the rest had been withdrawn from circulation, when the corrected edition, now submitted to the reader, was prepared. The various Poems and Dramas have received the author's most careful revision." Careful revision does not of course mean elaborate rewriting. The fragmentary *Saul* was published on the advice of Miss Barrett; it was later revised and lengthened into its present form.[21] The *Flight of the Duchess* was also published in fragmentary form in *Hood's Magazine* "in an emergency," and later expanded into its present form. *Paracelsus* underwent frequent revisions, and Browning made many minor omissions and additions. Nearly a third of the lines were changed at one time or another between 1835-1888, but a comparison of the first and last editions shows that the revisions were very slight.

> That, far from them.................(1835)

becomes

> That, when afar ....(1888)

> That's beautiful is one! and when he learns
> That every common sight he can enjoy. (1835)

becomes

> That's beauteous proves alike! When Festus
>   learns
> That every common pleasure of the world
>   (1888)

>   ....the last hopes I conceived
> Are fading even now. Old stories tell..(1835)

[21] A list of first readings is in H. E. Hersey's edition of *Christmas Eve and Easter Day and Other Poems.*

becomes

> I said my latest hope
> Is fading even now. A story tells.....(1888)

A few of the revisions are more drastic, usually, but not always, illustrating Browning's passion for compression, as when

> Alas! as I forbode, this weighty talk
> Has for its end no other than to revive. (1835)

becomes

> Once more? Alas! As I foretold......(1888)

and

> As you had your own soul: accordingly
> I could go further back, and trace each bough
> Of this wide-branching tree even to its birth;
> Each full-grown passion to its outspring faint;
> But I shall only dwell upon the intents
> Which filled you when,..............(1835)

becomes

> As you had your own soul and those intents
> Which filled it when,...............(1888)

These few typical examples must serve for many. They show us that in a youthful poem which he valued he would revise with considerable ruthlessness.[22] Even *Pauline* came in for minor revisions in the 1887 edition of his poems.[23]

Sordello, the other long poem of his youth, was also revised as it went through new editions in his collected works. But these revisions were less elaborate even than *Paracelsus,* and *Book II* remained unchanged. Unlike his changes in *Paracelsus,* these were, almost without a single exception, expansions of the earlier version, very probably due to the loud

---

[22] A convenient place to study the revision of *Paracelsus* and *Sordello* is G. W. Cook: *Browning Guide-Book,* pp. 265-279, where all the changes are reprinted. So far as I know there is no variorum Browning.

[23] The variant readings are reprinted in *Poet Lore,* 1:520.

criticisms of its extreme obscurity and compression, just as *Paracelsus* was criticized for its prolixity. He seriously considered rewriting the poem after Miss Barrett criticized the tenuous continuity of its parts; but he never got it done. He merely revised certain parts of it in the second edition, and added descriptive headings which help to bridge the gaps of obscurity. When he decided to revise it, he asked for his friend Domett's annotated copy of the poem. When the new edition appeared it had adopted Domett's marginal suggestions.[24] We may illustrate the kind of revision he made by a single example typical of all.

> And round those three the Peoples formed a ring,
> Suspended their own vengeance, chose await.... (1840)

becomes

> And round those three the people formed a ring,
> Of visionary judges whose award
> He recognized in full—faces that barred
> Henceforth return to the old careless life,
> In whose great presence, therefore, his first strife
> For their sakes must not be ignobly fought,
> All these at once approved of him, he thought,
> Suspended their own vengeance, chose await.. (1863)

Most of the changes were for the better, for Browning, while in the throes of composition, was not always delicately selective in his diction.

What care he did take in revision seems to have been largely due to the influence of Elizabeth Barrett. Her influence on his view of life and love has been often

---

[24] An example of the revision is given by Domett in the *Living Age*, 244:406. In the margin of the lines:

> ....gather fruits of one great gaze
> At the noon-sun: look you! The same orange haze,—
> The same blue stripe round that—and, i' the midst, . .
>   *Book I*, 579-581.

Domett had written after "At the noon-sun": "Rather the moon from the description"; and after "i' the midst": "Why cut off the 'n'?" Browning, who had borrowed Domett's copy of the poem, saw and adopted both suggestions; he added the 'n' and changed the "noon-sun" to the "moon."

observed; but her influence on the technical construction of his poetry was also tremendous. In his earlier years, Browning worked alone without the aid of association or advice of a fellow artist. Compared with a person like Addison, who always showed his work to several friends and scrupulously corrected and altered what they felt was wrong,[25] Browning was a literary hermit. He did not show his work to other people before publication until he met Elizabeth. That acquaintance began with an exchange of letters complimenting each other's poetry; but before many days it has ripened into friendly criticisms of each other's work. Browning begins immediately to expand under the loving warmth of her interest and her illuminating comments on his work, and with characteristic enthusiasm he begins to talk to her about poems under construction, and to seek her advice. This first emergence from his literary solitude is attended by a boyish self-consciousness. Writing to Elizabeth about the unfinished *Flight of the Duchess,* he says, "And *The Flight of the Duchess,* to leave nothing out, is only the beginning of a story written some time ago, and given to poor Hood in his emergency at a day's notice —the true stuff and story is all to come. . . it is one of my *Dramatic Romances.* So is a certain *Saul* I should like to show you one day—an ominous liking— for nobody ever sees what I do till it is printed. But as you *do* know the printed little part of me, I should not be sorry if, in justice, you knew all I have *really* done—written in the portfolio there—though that would be far enough from *this* me, that wishes to you now. I should like to write something in concert with you, how I would try." [26]

[25] Pope is responsible for this. Quoted in Spence's Anecdotes; Quoted as footnote in Thackeray, *English Humorists,* under Addison.
[26] *Letters,* Vol. I, p. 58.

It was under her influence that Browning first spoke out in his own person instead of making other people speak dramatically. He wrote, "You *do* what I always wanted, hoped to do, and only seem now likely to do for the first time. You speak out—*you*—I only make men and women speak—give you truth broken into prismatic hues. . ."[27] She wrote back that she wished he would write a poem not connected either directly or indirectly with the stage. Interestingly enough, in his next volume of *Bells and Pomegranates* (No. VII, 1845), the first volume of poems after his acquaintance with Elizabeth, we find that in fifteen of them he has spoken in his own person. All of his work previous to this date, with the possible exception of one or two short lyrics, are dramatic.

After the acquaintance grew intimate, we find in Browning a growing concern in his poetic diction, a constant reliance upon Miss Barrett for criticisms which were nearly always adopted. He revised his poems with some care before publication, and so did she. She went over his lines with minute care, pencil in hand, making corrections and suggestions.[28] He had the greatest confidence in her critical judgment. He kept revising *The Duchess* (as the *Letters* speak of it) with her counsel, until it met with her approval and she could write of it: "*The Duchess* appears to me more than ever a new-minted golden coin—the rhythm of it answering to your own description, 'Speech half asleep, or song half awake?' You have right of trove to these novel effects of rhythm."[29] He paid loving tribute to her for these criticisms, and his whole spirit might best be shown by this passage from one of his letters to her: "For the criticism itself, it is all true,

[27] *Ibid*, I, p. 6.
[28] *Letters*, especially Vol. I, pp. 148, 268, 138-9.
[29] *Ibid*. Vol. I, p. 253.

. . .—all the suggestions are to be adopted, the improvements accepted. I so thoroughly understand your spirit in this, that, just in this beginning, I should really like to have found some point in which I could cooperate with your intention, and help my work by disputing the effect of any alteration proposed, if it ought to be disputed—*that* would answer your purpose exactly as well as agreeing with you—so that the benefit to me were apparent; but this time I cannot dispute one point. All is for the best.

"So much for this *Duchess*—which I shall ever rejoice in—wherever was a bud, even, in that strip of May-bloom, a live musical bee hangs now. I shall let it lie (my poem), till just before I print it; and then go over it, alter at the places, and do something for the places where I (really) wrote anyhow, almost, to get done." [30]

It would be hard to imagine a better combination of talent: the strong masculine vigor of Browning's thought and phrases, skilfully refined by Miss Barrett's almost too feminine delicacy and prettiness. It is not without significance that the great lyrics and dramatic monologues were composed or refined under her influence; and that in these poems, in contrast to those of both his early and later periods, there is dominant a melody and a perfectness of poetic diction which Tennyson himself seldom surpassed.

In the years which followed Mrs. Browning's death, her critical function was carried on by Browning's French friend Milsand. The Browning who bashfully confesses to Elizabeth that no one ever sees the things he writes is not the same Browning who in later years leans heavily upon the advice of his foreign friend.

[30] *Letters*, vol. I, p. 138-9. Many of Browning's critics wondered if others were not written in the same way which escaped the notice of Elizabeth Barrett.

The following letter from Browning to Milsand is revealing. Under date of May 13, 1872, he writes:

DEAREST FRIEND:

The two proofs about which you inquire, the 'doubles' corrected, were sent inadvertently, I think: whenever you get the whole series, corrected, you will see for yourself . . . how *inestimable* your assistance has been. There is not one point to which you called attention which I was not thereby enabled to improve—in some cases essentially benefit. (He then speaks of his purpose to punctuate all his past work on the principle suggested by Milsand's corrections, and continues.) But the other changes and elucidations are of vital importance: you cannot think me so ignorant of what your purpose is in making a correction, that, if I found it, in my opinion, no improvement, I would adopt it all the same.

The fact is, in the case of a writer with my peculiarities and habits, somebody quite ignorant of what I may have meant to write, and only occupied with what is really written, ought to supervise the thing produced. And I never hoped or dreamed I should find such an intelligence as yours at my service....[31]

Here is Robert Browning gladly making any correction suggested by his friend, even when he does not regard it as an improvement; and seriously proposing to revise all his punctuations on some principle which Milsand has suggested!

But we would not make too much of this point. It should go without saying that he revised. The significant point for this study is that in comparison with other poets, Browning was unusually rapid in composition and usually reluctant in revision. With the exception of the lyrics revised in consultation with Elizabeth, his revisions were in the interest of clearness and accuracy rather than smoothness of rhythm or beauty of expression. These qualities, as we have seen, were not paramount in his theory of poetry, and

[31] Quoted, Thomas Bentzon: "A French Friend of Browning," *Scribner's*, 20:108ff.

he preferred conciseness to the long rhythmical periods of *Paradise Lost* which have usually been considered the glory of blank verse. There are, of course, other elements to be reckoned with in a study of the peculiarities of Browning's verse, but a knowledge of his methods of composition and revision helps us to understand some of the apparent roughness and uncouthness of his verse.

CHAPTER III

BROWNING'S EAR AND SENSE OF PATTERN

WHEN CHARLES LAMB exclaimed, "I have no ear," he unconsciously uttered a profound metrical truth; for human ears are not equally gifted with a sense of rhythm. Elia could neither sing, hum, nor whistle "God Save the King," and some intelligent people cannot become aware of a continuous metrical pattern in *A Grammarian's Funeral,* or give a satisfactory reading of *Saul* or of *Master Hugues of Saxe-Gotha.*

Some ears like to have the prose phrases coincide exactly with the metrical pattern, with the anvil ringing on every stress. They are pleased with,

> I have a boy of five years old;
> His face is fair and fresh to see;
> His limbs are cast in beauty's mould,
> And dearly he loves me.

Others apparently do not sense metrical patterns at all, and they anticipate no recurrence of time parts. They lift the prose phrases from the metrical frame, and, unconscious of the temporal uniformity of verse, read it as though it were badly printed prose. Who has not heard the following passage from *The Tempest* read thus:

I' the commonwealth I would by contraries execute all things; for no kind of traffic would I admit; no name of magistrate; letters should not be known; riches, poverty, and use of service, none;........

Still others are aggressively rhythmic in their feeling for time, and can sense a metrical pattern vividly enough to break up the most recalcitrant and unruly prose phrase into rhythmic units. The ear becomes adjusted and standardized to this pattern; it reaches on into the line with this expectancy, and finds what it expects. It takes pleasure in metrical experiments, and finds the same metrical pattern underneath such pertinacious phrases as,

Some parson, some smug crop-haired smooth-chinned sort.
(*Inn A.* 2.293)

and such frail cheese-cloth as,

Of feminine desirability. (*Inn A.* 2.205)

In the one it is able, by shifting the pitch on syllables of equal importance in meaning, to bring out the thought and at the same time satisfy the sense for pattern. In the other the sense of time runs on so lively and independently that the pattern is felt to exist in the ear of the reader even though it is not emphatically marked by stresses on every other syllable.

Browning is the great Cham of this third group, for he is an aggressive timer; one whose subjective sense of rhythm is so alert and robust that it arranges into sensibly equal time parts which are experienced as rhythmic any series or succession of sounds. He would hardly be pleased with the smooth cadence of, let us say, some of Robert Frost's verse where the lines have a colloquial ease of movement which suggests good prose without being opposed to monotonous regularity if your fancy directs or your physiology compels such a reading. Even Kipling's verse would not long please Browning, if we may judge from his own practice; for Kipling's phrases reinforce the metrical pattern so that it sings itself to the primitive beat of a tom-tom, while Browning's verse in the same patterns is relieved by the constant pull between the primitive

rhythm and the opposing phrases. He likes to lay violent hands upon rugged, prosaic phrases, and bend
them and break them and force them into patterns
which they do not naturally fit. This makes much of
his verse sound rough, often uncouth, especially to
unaggressive ears.

He composed with such ease and agility that he was
not fastidious in selecting his phrases, and he never
took what a poet like Tennyson would call scrupulous
pains with his versification. To use one of his own
phrases, he sometimes "hitches the thing into verse."
He considered versification "the mere outward crust"
of his thought, a consideration which seems to have
reminded many of his readers and critics that the crust
could be both hard and tough. An ear that can impose upon a rough series of syllables a regular metrical
pattern, as Browning could and did, does not make
much effort to write smooth lines in which the prose
accents are exactly coincident with the metrical
stresses. The subjective feeling for pattern makes its
objective presence seem less important.

One is irresistably drawn toward the supposition
that there must be a causal connection between his
personality and his prosody. For he was vigorous and
full of a restless and exuberant energy. He was pas-
sionately in love with life and its activity. While
Tennyson sat and smoked, or moved solemnly and
thoughtfully about his garden, Browning would bound
up the steps two at a time, crush a flower in his im-
patience to discover its soul, or rush to the opposite
end of the city to keep a social engagement. His verse
reflects the same rugged personality, the same over-
flowing energy.

He read his verse, not in a chanting monotone like
Tennyson or Rossetti, but dramatically with energetic

observance of time; thundering out the *Song of David* of Christopher Smart, tenderly restraining the accents in *Pompilia,* and beating out the time of *Echetlos* by stamping his foot on the stresses.[1]   He must have felt the same way when he wrote, stamping his foot subjectively while he metered his lines as he did objectively when he read them.   It is impossible to read some of them without following his example. Except when he made a mistake, which was seldom indeed, the pattern is there struggling out of the prose phrasing if you can twist your thumbs in opposite directions, stamp your foot, and find it.

His many triple and quadruple movements are good illustrations of this aggressive sense of pattern.   The metre of *Saul* is hardly mistakable in the first line.

Said Abner, "At last thou art come! Ere I tell, ere thou speak,

and is unequivocal in lines like these:

And I bent once again to my playing, pursued it un-
    checked, (67)
Made a proffer of good to console him—he slowly resumed (207)

Poems written in this anapestic movement usually fall into an annoying sing-song, as *The Old Oaken Bucket* and the anapestic poems of Byron and Bryant have shown; for the phrases coincide exactly with the metrical pattern.   Browning, however, as preliminary steps toward making the movement pleasing to his ear, adds a fifth measure to Byron's "Ye scenes of my childhood, whose loved recollection," then rhymes in couplets and eschews feminine endings.   He carefully restrains his prose phrasings from reinforcing the pattern and keeps them straining against its bonds, so that many of the lines must be marked and stamped

[1] Sidney Colvin: Some Personal Recollections: "Rossetti and Browning." *Scribner's,* Vol. 61, 1920.

before they can be read. But despite the conflict he could feel the pattern in

Death was past, life not come: so he waited. Awhile his right
      hand
Held the brow, helped the eyes left too vacant forthwith to re-
      mand (119-20)

and at the same time give "death," "life," "right," "helped," their proper emphasis. He could write,

I repórt, as a mán may of Gód's work—all's lóve, yet all's láw.
                              (242)

and feel the temporal importance of "man," and "God's," as well as the sense importance of "may," and "work." I venture that any other poet of the century would have written,

I repórt, as man máy of God's wórk—all is lóve, yet all's láw.

Tennyson wrote *Locksley Hall* in smooth, restrained phrases which cling flexibly to the metrical pattern like a smile to the lips; and as one reads, the metre looks after itself.

Many a night I saw the Pleiads, rising thro' the mellow shade,
Glitter like a swarm of fireflies tangled in a silver braid.

The phrases do not pull against the metre, the long line drops lazily sometimes into two four-measure lines, often into one four-measure line in four-four time, and the thought is usually completed in a coup-let. But Browning, in *La Saisiaz* and *Clive*, which are in the same metre, seldom allows his phrases to rest at ease with the pattern. He avoids the easy four-plus-four, with phrases either shorter or longer than expected; and instead of ending a thought in a couplet, he allows it to run on through several lines. Still the aggressive timing ear will hear the *Locksley Hall* pattern in,

Till the landing on the staircase saw escape the latest spark:
"Sleep you well!" "Sleep but as well, you!"—lazy love
         quenched, all was dark.   (81-82)

and

Splintered in the slab, this pink perfection of the cyclamen;
Scarce enough to heal and coat with amber gum the sloe-tree's
         gash,   (16-17)

The metre of *A Grammarian's Funeral* is often considered difficult, but beautiful and strange.   It is another instance of Browning's aggressive timing.   The long lines are pentameter couplets which fit into *Sordello* without disturbance; they show no variation not common to it, but they have a heavy proportion of direct-attack lines and weak stresses which, through repetition, tend to set up a new rhythm.   The short lines are adonics so familiar in the *Odes* of Horace.[2] Each line by itself, or the long lines taken together, are simple enough; it is the combination that is complex.   For the high percentage of direct-attack lines with adonics between tends to confuse some ears which do not go easily from one to the other.   Even Browning himself may not have entirely escaped the difficulty when he was writing them.

Master Hugues of Saxe-Gotha even more clearly illustrates this aggression which imposes upon obstreperous words a metrical pattern.   The metre will break down on the reader who cannot stamp his foot, actually or figuratively, and the meaning will vanish

---

[2] Mercuri, facunde nepos Atlantis,
   qui feros cultus hominum recentum
   voce formasti catus at decorae
      more palaestrae,   (Bk. I, Ode X)

for who cannot syncopate the prose accents over the strong beat of the metre. Browning, apparently, could do both, and found great delight in,

> Hugues! I advise *meâ poenâ*
> (Counterpoint glares like a Gorgon)
> Bid One, Two, Three, Four, Five, clear the arena!
> Say the word, straight I unstop the full organ,
> Blare out the *mode Palestrina.*

He was subjectively so conscious of his pattern that he often failed to make it clear to the reader in the opening lines of his poems. His generous critic Elizabeth Barrett remonstrated with him against this perversity in these words:

> "And the 'Laboratory' is hideous as you meant to make it:— only I object a little to your tendency. . . which is almost a habit, and is very observable in this poem I think, . . . of making lines difficult for the reader to read . . . see the opening lines of this poem. Not that music is required everywhere, nor in *them* certainly, but that the uncertainty of rhythm throws the reader's mind off the *rail.* . . and interrupts his progress with you, and your influence with him." [3]

The confusing beginning is,

> Now that I, tying thy glass mask tightly,
> May gaze through these faint smokes curling whitely,
> As thou pliest thy trade in this devil's-smithy—
> Which is the poison to poison her, prithee?

where no two lines are the same.

He never reformed. He boomed out the measures of *Echetlos* when he wrote them, but at what point is the reader certain of the pattern? On first examination the first three lines seem to have nothing in common, and not until the fourth line does the reader

[3] *Letters*, Vol. I, p. 135. (Letter for July 21, 1845.)

recognize any striking similarity in the metre. It is like the second.

Here is a story shall stir you! Stand up, Greeks dead and gone,
Who breasted, beat Barbarians, stemmed Persia rolling on,
Did the deed and saved the world, for the day was Marathon!

No man but did his manliest, kept rank and fought away
In his tribe and file: up, back, out, down—was the spear-arm
      play:
Like a wind-swept branchy wood, all spear-arms a-swing that
      day!

But one man kept no rank, and his sole arm plied no spear,
As a flashing came and went, and a form i' the van, the rear,
Brightened the battle up, for he blazed now there, now here.

The sixth and seventh are new, the eighth is like the third (except for an extra syllable), the ninth is new, etc.

The line is loosely designed, but it is always divided into two parts of three measures each, which may be either duple or triple. It may begin with direct attack, or with a single or double anacrusis.

But there is no end to the illustrations of this fundamental consideration of Browning's prosody. It should be clear, however, that Browning not only had an ear, but a very unusual one for a poet. It leapt lightly over combinations of sounds which gave pause to less aggressive ears, and took delight in lines which must be subdued and conquered by a strong subjective feeling for pattern. This fact is the key to many of the peculiarities and much of the individuality of Browning's verse.

PART TWO

CHAPTER IV

BROWNING'S BLANK VERSE: GENERAL CHARACTERISTICS

TWO THIRDS of Browning's enormous quantity of verse is written in unrhymed pentameters. And if the volume is amazing, its flexibility is no less so. It ranges in theme from the confession and defense of Mr. Sludge, to that of the gentle Pompilia; from the character drama of an old roué in the *Inn Album,* to the search for the ultimate in *Paracelsus;* from the theology of *Cleon* to that of *Caliban;* from *Ned Bratts* to *Andrea del Sarto.* The versification is somewhat different in each poem, as if the author had tried to adapt his medium to his characters, but this dramatic appropriateness is very rudimentary, and he would be a bold man who tried to explain Browning's verse on that assumption. But it does have a tremendous range in music through all the variant chords from the strains of exalted beauty in

> O lyric Love, half angel and half bird
> And all a wonder and a wild desire,—
> Boldest of hearts that ever braved the sun,
> Took sanctuary within the holier blue,
> And sang a kindred soul out to his face,—
> Yet human at the red-ripe of the heart—
> (*R&B* 1.1383-88)

to the scabrous discords of

> And did I spoil sport, pull face grim,—nay, grave?
> Your pupil does you better credit! No!
> I parleyed with my pass-book,—rubbed my pair
> At the big balance in my banker's hands,—
> Folded a cheque cigar-case-shape,—just wants

> Filling and signing,—and took train, resolved
> To execute myself with decency
> And let you win—if not Ten thousand quite,
> Something by way of wind-up-farewell burst
> Of firework-nosegay!   (*Inn Album* 1.208-217)

On all too few occasions it can sweep into the full
organ with tones not unworthy of Milton at some
moments, as in the passage in *Aristophanes' Apology*
which ends:

> What if thy watery plural vastitude,
> Rolling unanimous advance, had rushed,
> Might upon might, a moment,—stood, one stare,
> Sea-face to city-face, thy glaucous wave
> Glassing that marbled last magnificence,—
> Till fate's pale tremulous foam-flower tipped the gray,
> And when wave broke and overswarmed and, sucked
> To bounds back, multitudinously ceased,
> Let land again breathe unconfused with sea,
> Attiké was, Athenai was not now!   (20-29)

And perhaps on too many occasions it can fall into
feeble, high-pitched pipings like those of the Pope:

> Civilization and the Emperor
> Succeed to Christianity and the Pope.
> One Emperor then, as one Pope now: meanwhile,
> Anticipate a little! We tell thee "Take
> Guido's life, sapped society shall crash,
> Whereof the main prop was, is, and shall be
> —Supremacy of husband over wife!"
>   (*R&B* 10.2023-29)

It slides from such elephantine lines as:

> He hath watched hunt with that slant white-wedge eye.
>   (*Caliban* 49)

to such frail invertebrates as:

> Incontrovertably. Theodoric, (*R&B* 8.474)

There is a certain dramatic propriety in this range
which helps to justify it and which eases the reader

over what he would otherwise object to as prosaic if not actually bad verse. The other explanatory element, as we have seen, is Robert Browning.

His urge toward poetry was born to his admiration of Shelley who had set fire to his youthful imagination, and *Pauline* was its first fruit. Its metre is as much the shadow of Shelley as its theme.

The most characteristic type of line in Shelley's poetry is:

Made paler the pale moon, to her cold home. (*Alastor* 138)

where the important adjectives are emphasized by making monosyllabic measures of them preceding their nouns. These lines are pleasing to the ear in verse of restrained sentiment, for they put little strain upon the iambic pattern. The young poet catches the tune from his idol, and writes lines on the same model:

The wind murmuring in the damp copse. (*Pauline* 66)

Occasionally he catches the lyric note on a Shelley tune, and writes a passage like:

Thou wilt remember one warm morn when winter
Crept aged from the earth, and spring's first breath
Blew soft from the moist hills; the blackthorn boughs,
So dark in the bare wood, when glistening
In the sunshine were white with coming buds,
Like the bright side of a sorrow, and the banks
Had violets opening from sleep like eyes.
I walked with thee who knew'st not a deep shame.........
                                             (*Pauline* 55-62)

Six of these lines use the adjectives after the manner of Shelley, and the resulting movement is like that of *Alastor*. In fact, the percentage of such lines is the same in each poem—an average of twenty to the hundred lines. Later, when he flames into his own orbit, lines of this type are not conspicuous in his versification.

But although *Pauline* is full of these echoes from another poet; although the metrical features of monosyllabic measures and weak stresses are frequently imitative, there are in this first poem arresting evidences of an embryo Browning who delights in smashing the regularity of the metrical pattern with lines full of rebellion and unexpectedness. He probably learned them from no master.

Who has deceived God,—if such one should seek (23)
In the sunshine were white with coming buds, (59)
Drawing me to thee—these build up a screen (4)
Since all the wandering and all the weakness (125)
Scarce worth a moth's flitting, which long grasses cross
(173)

Of his next effort, *Paracelsus,* the Athenaeum said that "it was not without talent, but spoiled by obscurity and only an imitation of Shelley." There is without doubt considerable truth in the statement, but the imitation of Shelley is more in its mood than in metre. The mental drama rather than the outward events gives the prevailing tone to it which tranquilizes the movement of the verse. It hasn't a single "o' the," and only one "i' the." The verse is calm, monotonously uniform if the later verse sets the standard, and without the compression of the more vigorous monologues. The easy movement of the lines leads him into the prolixity which he tried to compress in the later revisions. He depended for variation upon feminine endings, of which there is one in every ten lines (more than in any other of his poems), and upon the double anacrusis, which is usually an extra syllable and not the result of a monosyllabic first-measure as in Shelley. Triple measures, so prominent in the later poems, are not frequent; many long passages are almost unbroken in their regularity.

These first efforts are subdued, and flavored with a romantic *Weltschmerz* from which the later Browning is free. The versification has something of the same quality, if versification may be considered as romantic. It is not yet the instrument of the great monologues; its tones are still feeble, and its range is limited. But this is only 1835, and the poet is twenty-three. The next ten years are full of the eight dramas which exacted of him strict discipline in the dramatic method. At the end of this apprenticeship, Browning has grown into his full poetic stature; he has become a master in his own right with a method as individual as its subject. He has burst full-grown into the Browning of *Men and Women* (184-, 5-).

There were important developments during those ten years. The subdued tones of *Pauline* are gone, and in their place are the dramatic passions, the self-revealing speeches, the broken phrases and colloquial ejaculations of the characters in the drama, who speak with increasing ease and freedom. There is also a growing roughness in the metre, due in part to the explosive character of the speeches, in part to the expanding sense of freedom in the blank-verse medium.

> Oh, where's the King's heir?—Gone!—the Crown Prince?
> Gone!
> Where's Savoy? Gone!—Sardinia? Gone! But Charles
> Is left!
>
>   *   *   *   *
>
>   Oh worst, worst, worst of all!
> Tell me! What, Victor? He has made you King?
> What's he then? What's to follow this? You, King?
>
>   (*King Victor and King Charles*)
>   (II. 339-41; 350-52)

The weak feminine endings were discarded at the end of this dramatic apprenticeship. Prior to *Luria* these endings were a characteristic feature of Browning's versification; in *Pauline, Paracelsus,* and the early dramas they had occurred at the comparatively high rate of from five to ten per cent. In *Luria,* the last of the dramas, they fall to four per cent, and they all but disappear in *Men and Women* where five of the nine blank-verse poems have none at all, three have less than one per cent, and *Fra Lippo Lippi* has 1.57. He never returned to them as a metrical device.[1]

There is no sudden leap from the dramas to the dramatic monologues; rather the one shades into the other, for the monologues are simply little dramas in which only one of the actors speaks. Browning found this form more congenial to his talents than conventional drama, and cultivated it continuously to the end of his days.

The peculiarity of his blank verse is due largely to the exacting demands of the dramatic monologue for which it was cultivated. And Browning was fully aware of these demands. He speaks of them frequently in his letters to Miss Barrett, recognizing the limitations imposed by the medium, and the artistic difficulties which must be overcome. In one of his earliest letters he writes, "You speak out, *you*—I only make men and women speak—give you truth broken into prismatic hues. . ."[2] In another letter he compared the work of the novelist with that of the poet. "And what easy work these novelists have of it! A Dramatic poet has to *make* you love or admire his men

[1] For a complete table of the English Poets' use of the feminine ending see Morton: *The Technique of English Non-Dramatic Blank Verse.* Chicago, 1910.

[2] *Letters,* Vol. I, page 6.

and women—they must *do* and *say* all that you are to
see and hear—really do it in your face, say it in your
ears, and it is wholly for *you*, in *your* power, to name,
characterize and so praise or blame, *what* is so said
and done. . . if you don't perceive of yourself, there
is no standing by, for the Author, and telling you. But
with the novelist, a scrape of the pen—out blurting of
a phrase, and the miracle is achieved—'Consuelo possessed to perfection this and the other gift'—what
would you more?" [3]

It would tax one to state more specifically the demands of the monologue. Here for an instant the spot
light is turned upon some soul in a critical moment;
and in that instant the situation must be presented,
the supposed audience or partners to the drama must
be introduced (for although they are necessary to the
situation they are never actually in focus), the motiva-
tion and course of the action must be made clear—all
in the uninterrupted monologue of a single character
who is painting his own picture while he speaks. These
are heavy demands, and in order to meet them, Browning resorts to interjections, replies, and rejoinders
which all but introduce dialogue; artful phrases, ex-
plosives, parenthetical asides, ellipses, short broken
sentences which reveal character and situation; all of
which help to give the lines their Browningesque color.
With these stylistic tricks he could build a monologue
so skillfully that the police and the compromising
neighborhood are as vivid as Lippo himself; or that
a minute character sketch could be written of the un-
seen and unheard Elvire in *Fifine at the Fair*. The
metre is almost always choppy, and never soars into
long passages of Miltonic harmony. But then one is
not likely to speak in Miltonic periods when rough

[3] *Letters*, Vol. I, page 155.

hands are fiddling on one's throat in a dark street at midnight!

From *Transcendentalism* to *Imperante Augusto,* Browning's blank verse bears the stamp imprinted by the method of the dramatic monologue. With few exceptions the metre is rough and often rebellious in the restraint of the pattern. In many instances this seems to be by design; but dramatic appropriateness of language is one of Browning's accomplishments only within certain wide limits. The versification of *Cleon* is different from that of *Caliban*—one is smooth and restrained, the other is more primitive and strains against the iambic pattern; *Pompilia* is quiet and modulated, *Sludge* and *Blougram* are vulgar and explosive; *The Pope* is thoughtful soliloquy. But not one of them is free from Browning's peculiarity of speech, despite his dramatic detachment. And in the later poems, there is no differentiation at all, as an illustration from the *Inn Album* will show:

THE BOY:
> Does he believe I fail to comprehend
> He wants just one more final friendly snack
> At friend's exchequer ere friend runs to earth,
> Marries renounces yielding friends such sport?'
>   (*Inn A.* 1.204-7)

THE MAN:
> "*I* polished snob off to aristocrat?
> You compliment me! father's apron still
> Sticks out from son's court-vesture: still silk purse
> Roughs finger with some bristle sow-ear-born!
>   (1.395-8)
> I ended just by knocking head against
> That plaguy low-hung branch yourself began
> By getting bump from; as at last you too
> May stumble o'er that stump which first of all
> Bade me walk circumspectly.
>   (2.129-134)

THE GIRL:

> Do you remember, at the library
> We saw together somewhere, those two books
> Somebody said were noticeworthy? One
> Lay wide on table, sprawled its painted leaves
> For all the world's inspection; shut on shelf
> Reclined the other volume, closed, clasped, locked,—
> Clear to be let alone.
>
> (3.199-205)

THE WOMAN:

> You bid break trust,
> This time, with who trusts me,—not simply bid
> Me trust you, me who ruined but myself,
> In trusting but myself!
>
> (4.653-6)

THE AUTHOR:

> Wicks are noisome-deep
> In wax, to detriment of plated ware;
>
> (1.96-7)
>
> They slacken pace: the younger stops abrupt,
> Discards cigar, looks his friend full in face.
>
> (2.16-17)

From his early beginning as an admirer and imitator of Shelley, through *Paracelsus* to the dramas, he grows into his mastery of his own type of blank verse, which is already full grown in *Men and Women*. What, then, were the metrical principles upon which this verse was built?

A close and sometimes painful study of his practice reveals but two metrical rules from which he is never known to depart:

1—A blank verse line must contain not less than nine, nor more than fifteen syllables!

2—It must not have less than two heavily stressed syllables nor more than ten!

The one exception to the first rule is clearly an accident or an oversight:

Till Rome, that Rome whereof—this voice (*R&B* 9.721)

Nine-syllable lines are not common, but they do occur:

Steadied him a moment, set him straight (*R&B* 4.289)
And in your name? I presume so much, (*R&B* 7.1359)
Plainly, and need so be put aside: (*R&B* 11.518)

Eleven- and twelve- syllable lines are not uncommon in any English blank verse, but many of the poets had in mind certain rules of elision with which to justify them. There is no evidence that Browning had any rules of elision at all. Thirteen-syllable lines are very common in Browning:

This being a fatherly pat o' the cheek, no more. (*R&B* 4.1254)
Francesca Camilla Vittoria Angela (*R&B* 7.6)
And Judge the Other, with even—a word and a wink (*R&B* 4.52)
From the terrible patience of God? "All which just means,
(*R&B* 11.1376)
I' the matrimonial thrust and parry, at least (*R&B* 4.547)
Like the skipping of rabbits by moonlight,—three slim shapes.
(*Fra Lippo* 59)

Fourteen-syllable lines are occasional:

O' the baker or candlestick-maker? In all the rest (*R&B* 4.590)
The aim o' the cruelty being so crueller still, (*R&B* 4.684)
By comers and goers in Via Vittoria: eh? (*R&B* 3.74)

Fifteen-syllables are infrequent:

O' the "Great and Terrible Name"? Shall the Heaven of
Heavens (*Sludge* 1074)

To speak in terms of stresses, a line may have from two to ten, but there are few clear cases of ten full stresses.

There may be two stresses: i.e. three light ones must be added.

Historical and philosophical (*Red C. N. C. C.* 3.762)
Unlimited in capability (*Cleon* 326)
Incontrovertibly. Theodoric, (*R&B* 8.474)
Civilization and the Emperor (*R&B* 10.2023)

There may be three stresses: i.e. two light ones must be added.

At the Strozzi, at the Pillar, at the Bridge;	(*R&B* 1.110)
Setebos, Setebos, and Setebos!	(*Caliban* 24)
To account for the thawing of an icicle,	(*R&B* 4.857)
Impotent, penniless and miserable!	(*R&B* 4.923)
To error in a woman and a wife,	(*R&B* 9.848)

There may be four stresses: (with or without the light stress.)

'Thinketh, He dwelleth i' the cold o' the moon.	(*Caliban* 25)
Followed her parents i' the face o' the world,	(*R&B* 3.720)
But flirting flag-like i' the face o' the world	(*R&B* 3.888)

There may be six stresses: i.e. one not required by the metre:

—Terni's fall, Naples' bay and Gothard's top—(*Blougram* 533)
Prayers move God; threats, and nothing else, move men!
(*R&B* 7.1608)
The poor,—toils, moils and grinds the mill nor means
(*Inn Album* 6.113)
And broad-edge bold-print posters by the wall.
(*How It Strikes* 29)
Of some tongue-leaved eye-figured Eden tree, (*R&B* 3.235)

There may be seven stresses: i.e. two not required by the metre:

Be thou to me law, right, wrong, heaven and hell!
(*R&B* 11.2180)
With my poor young good beauteous murdered wife:
(*R&B* 11.1821)
There was a ripe round long black toothsome fruit,
(*R&B* 7.816)
Head-doubts, heart-doubts, doubts at my fingers' ends,
(*Blougram* 611)
And fruit, three red halves of starved winter-pears,
(*How It Strikes* 85)

There may be eight stresses: i.e. three not required by the metre:

If some flax-polled soft-bearded sire be found,   (*R&B* 9.44)
The one-arched brown brick bridge yawns over,—yes,
                                                  (*R&B* 11.9)
Or else stop race you boast runs neck and neck, (*R&B* 10.1581)
Some parson, some smug crop-haired smooth-chinned sort
                                          (*Inn Album* 2.293)
He hath watched hunt with that slant white-wedge eye
                                              (*Caliban* 49)
O' the first young girl's hand and the first old fool's purse!
                                              (*R&B* 5.450)

There may be nine stresses: i.e. four not required by the metre:

To these stout tall rough bright-eyed, black-haired boys,
                                             (*R&B* 10.929)
The hoarse shrill throat, see shut eyes, neck shot-forth,
                                             (*R&B* 8.234)
Whence, then, this quite new quick cold thrill,—cloudlike,
                                            (*R&B* 10.1248)
While-see how this mere chance-sown, cleft-nursed seed,
                                            (*R&B* 10.1036)
Who breaks law, breaks pact therefore, helps himself
                                            (*R&B* 11.523)

There may be ten stresses: i.e. five not required by the metre:

Fare ill, lie hard, lack clothes, lack fire, lack food? (*R&B* 4.645)

It is clear, then, and will be clearer still, that Browning was not greatly burdened with rules about the number of syllables a line may have, or about elisions, "substitutions," stresses, etc. He does none of these things according to any fixed rule. A line may have all the syllables it can carry; there may or may not be elision in lines of more than ten syllables; any meas-

ure may be monosyllabic; any syllable may carry the
prose or the metrical accent. He had a notion that
a blank-verse line should satisfy the ear's anticipation
of five measures; he also knew or unconsciously proved
that ears are unscientific and accept approximations
to the pattern of anticipation which the metre sets up.
Browning was pleased with a continuous variation
from this expected pattern. His ear accepted some
fourscore combinations which differ in some way from
the pattern of iambic pentameter. That is close to the
mathematical limit of possible variations, and it is not
surprising that Tennyson refused to read them because
he could not "put up with obsolete horrors and un-
rhythmical composition" through a "volume of
spasms." [4] But of course Tennyson is merely confess-
ing that his own margin of expectancy was much more
limited than that of Browning, who allowed himself
the latitude of nearly every type of blank verse line
since Surrey.

The number of different types of variations, however, taken as a fact by itself, is less significant than
the frequency with which these occur. Tennyson has
a variety of lines which seriously strain the metrical
pattern of blank verse, but little attention is paid to
them because they are rare. It is the frequency of
their occurrence and the proximity of a variety of
types to each other, as well as the excessive number
of them in Browning's verse, that make them bulk so
large in the reader's mind. Poets are usually careful
to preserve the normal pattern before and after a line
of doubtful conformity. But Browning was careless
of this. Sometimes he writes line after line of blank
verse which varies from the pattern, and temporarily

[4] Tennyson to Mrs. Brotherton. *Tennyson And His Friends*. Macmillan,
1912.

destroys it so that the reader does not know what to expect. Thus:

> "Thus it happed not, since thus he did the deed,
> And proved himself thereby portentousest
> Of cutthroats and a prodigy of crime,
> As the woman that he slaughtered was a saint,
> Martyr and miracle!" quoth the other to match:
> Again, more witness, and the case postponed.
>   (*R&B* 1.201-6)

Or to illustrate with a different type of variation:

> Sooner? What's soon or late i' the case?—ask we.
> A wound i' the flesh no doubt wants prompt redress;
> It smarts a little today, well in a week,
> Forgotten in a month; or never, or now, revenge!
> But a wound to the soul? That rankles worse and worse.
>   (*R&B* 4.1520-24)
> Leaving the shows of things to the Lord of Show
> And Prince o' the Power of the Air. Our very flight,
> Even to its most ambiguous circumstance,
> Irrefragably proved how futile, false. . .
> Why, men—men and not boys—boys and not babes—
> Babes and not beasts—beasts and not stocks and stones!—
>   (*R&B* 6.1793-1798)

The variations have a strong tendency to occur in clusters, as if the swing established itself in the poet's mind so strongly that it formed for the nonce the accepted pattern. Now a double anacrusis or a direct attack is a variation so trivial as to be all but unnoticed. But let these occur in line after line and there is a new norm established. These repetitions are frequent in Browning's verse. Here are two illustrations which could be indefinitely extended.

> The gratitude, forsooth, of a prostitute
> *To the* greenhorn and the bully—friends of hers,
> *From the* wag that wants the queer jokes for his club,
> *To the* snuff-box-decorator, honest man, . . .
>   (*Sludge* 783-86)

Doctor Bottini,—to no matter who,
Writes on the Monday two days afterward.
Now shall the honest championship of right,
Crowned with success, enjoy at last, unblamed,
Moderate triumph!
                           (*R&B* 12.390-394)

In the early poems even the feminine ending may occur frequently enough to affect the pattern, as,

They will not let me even die. Spare, spare *me,*
Sinning or no, forget that, only spare *me*
The horrible scorn! You thought I could support *it.*
But now you see what silly fragile crea*ture*
Cowers thus.
                           (*Paracelsus* 5.315-19)

That truth is just as far from me as ev*er;*
That I have thrown my life away; that sor*row*
On that account is idle, and further ef*fort*
To mend and patch what's marred beyond repair*ing,*
And useless: . . .
                           (*Paracelsus* 3.502-6)

It is no different with the triple measures. One triple in a line is not remarkable; even two of them may not be startling. But if these recur every few lines, as they do in Browning, they begin to strain the pattern; and if several successive lines have one or more triples, a new duple-triple movement is established. There are many such passages in Browning's blank verse.

And if they recog*nized in a critical* flash
From the zenith, each the *other, her* need of him,
His need of. . . say, a *woman to* perish for,
The *regular way o' the* world yet break no vow,
Do no harm save to himself,—if this were thus?
                           (*R&B* 3.1041-45)

Here he has Cardinal This to *vouch for the past,*
Cardinal That to *trust for the* future,—match
And marriage were a *Cardinal's making,—in short,*
What if a tragedy be acted here
Impossible for malice to improve,
And *innocent* Guido with his *innocent* four
                           (*R&B* 4.1599-1604)

The actual time of these measures is, approximately at least, the same; they might be written:

And | if they | recog | nized in a | critical | flash
 2 | 3   3 | 3 3 | 3 1½ 1½ | 2 2 2 | 4

But the introduction of one or more triples into any line temporarily breaks the iambic movement. That is, of course, the metrical reason for them—they preserve the time length of the measure which the ear demands, and at the same time give, as Poe said, "the agreeable variation of three syllables instead of the uniform two." If they occur too often (and they do sometimes in Browning's verse) they become the "uniform three," and a new movement is set up—a dupletriple, something like that of *Up In a Villa.*

Again, the failing stress on the sixth syllable is common to all blank verse, or any iambic pentameter line. It is more conspicuous on this syllable because it tends to shorten the line into four measures by hurrying over the third one, as,

Moreover Prosper and Miranda sleep   (*Caliban* 20)
Flat on his belly in the pit's much mire,   (*Caliban* 2)

where the weak stress is preceded by an easily elided syllable. Such lines are acceptable in tetrameter verse. But if these lines occur too often, as in *Caliban,* they become a characteristic feature of the verse, and if they begin to appear in succession the sense of the iambic pattern is dulled, or even lost. It is here that Browning's practice becomes important; he writes them in a series in a new pattern in the midst of iambic pentameter lines.

Setebos, Setebos, and Setebos!
'Thinketh, He dwelleth i' the cold o' the moon.
Thinketh He made it, with the sun to match.
                                    (*Caliban* 24-26)

As we stood listening on a sunny mound
To the wind murmuring in the damp copse,
Like heavy breathings of some hidden thing (*Pau.* 65-7)

That bloated bubble, with her soul inside,
Back to Arezzo and a palace there—
Or say, a fissure in the honest earth . . . (*R&B* 1.551-3)

Browning's work is full of lines made up of many weak stresses. A single line of this kind is not unusual in blank verse; the ear is often relieved by the frailty of such lines as,

Civilization is imperative.   (*R&B* 10.2012)

or by the dipodic flight of a line like

At the Strozzi, at the Pillar, at the bridge; (*R&B* 1.110)

But if a whole series of these lines gains no strength, the metre succumbs from the want of a backbone. Such passages are unaccountably frequent and long in Browning, especially in the later work. Open the blank-verse poems at random and find examples. Thus:

For Blougram, he believed, say, half he spoke.
The other portion, as he shaped it thus
For argumentatory purposes,
He felt his foe was foolish to dispute. (*Blougram* 980-3)

Name me, a primitive religionist—
As should the aboriginary be
I boast myself, Etruscan, Aretine,

    . . .   .
With,—for a visible divinity,—
The portent of a Jove Aegiochus
Descried 'mid clouds, lightning and thunder, couched
On topmost crag of your Capitoline:
                    (*R&B* 11.1913-5, 1918-21)
For, curiosity—how natural!
Importunateness—what a privilege
In the ardent sex!   (*R&B* 9.745-7)

> So did his cruelty burn life about,
> And lay the ruin bare in dreadfulness,
> Try the persistency of torment so
> Upon the wife, that, at extremity, . . .
>
> (*R&B* 10.629-32)

> Thus the man,—
> So timid when the business was to touch
> The uncertain order of humanity,
> Imperil, for a problematic cure
> Of grievance on the surface, any good
> I' the deep of things, dim yet discernible—
> This same man, so irresolute before, . . .
>
> (*Prince H-S* 1513-19)

> If petulant remonstrance made appeal,
> Unseasonable, o'erprotracted,—if
> Importunate challenge taxed the public ear
> When silence more decorously had served
> For protestation, . . .
>
> (*R&B* 9.260-4)

Browning had early in his career given up the use of the feminine ending, but in its stead is a growing percentage of lines ending on a weak syllable, as,

I hold a heavier fault imputable	(*R&B* 10.267)
Didst ever touch such ampollosity	(*R&B* 12.644)
And morning church is obligatory:	(*Inn A.* 1.181)
Pursuing chemistry or botany	(*Ibid* 1.297)
Your secret of superiority.	(*Ibid* 1.436)
Of feminine desirability,	(*Ibid* 2.205)
At the very purest, so compensating	(*Prince H-S.* 1327)
The superfluity of naughtiness,	(*R&B* 4.653)
And, reinaugurated, miracle	(*Red C. N. C. C.* 2.181)

For every one of Browning's heavy lines, gormandized with extra syllables and accents, and rebelling against the metrical pattern, there is one of these puny lines perishing from famine. In some of the poems there are so many of them that their effect is open to serious objection.

Strange as it may at first sound, lines made up wholly of monosyllables are a feature of Browning's verse. If it is true, as Gascoigne said, that "the more monosyllables you use, the truer Englishman shall you seem," Browning is the most English of the poets. Even Wordsworth is not a serious rival except when he actually attempts to reproduce the speech of the rustics as in *Michael* (ll.385-90). A single line of monosyllabic words might escape notice. But if two or three lines in succession are wholly monosyllabic and are followed immediately by still more, they become a stylistic trait which reacts sharply upon the versification.

For polysyllabic words are usually divided between two measures so that the metre slips on easily from one measure to the next, or, as is usually the case in Browning's verse, they give a trochaic trip to the metre.

> Rejecting past example, practice, precept, (*Par.* 1.415)

> And marble's language, Latin pure, discreet,
> (*Bish. Or. T.* 98)

> For riches, honor, pleasure, work, repose, (*Blougram* 280)

> The very Pandulph Shakespeare's fancy made,
> (*Blougram* 521)

> Some benediction anciently thy smile. (*R&B* 1.1401)

> O' the youthful, earnest, passionate—genius, beauty,
> (*Sludge* 1424)

But monosyllables often do not flow smoothly into each other; they maintain stubbornly their independence. The result is frequently rough, jerky, deterrent verse. The smooth vowels are lost in the rough em-

brace of bristly consonants which sharply divide each
word from its neighbor, as

> The hoarse shrill throat, see shut eyes, neck shot-forth,
> (*R&B* 8.234)
> The one-arched brown brick bridge yawns over—yes,
> (*R&B* 11.9)

It is difficult to preserve unharmed the metrical pattern amid such strife.   These examples are extreme,
of course, but one has only to turn to the poems for
overwhelming evidence of the frequency and the effect
of monosyllables in Browning's verse.   In *Bishop
Blougram's Apology* there is a passage of eighteen
lines (834-852) which has an average of nine words
to a line.   All through the poem, as in *Cleon, An Epistle, The Inn Album,* etc., etc., are swarms of them.

> See the world
> Such as it is,—you made it not, nor I;
> I mean to take it as it is,—and you,
> Not so you'll take it,—though you get naught else.
> (*Blougram* 230-233)
> More
> I think about and less I like the thing—
> No, you must let me!   Now, be good for once!
> . . .   .
> We played for love, not hate: yet, hate!   I hate. . .
> I had the cash
> To lose—you knew that!—lose and none the less
> Whistle tomorrow: . . .
> (*Inn Album* 2.22-24, 26, 29-31)

Or to take an example in which a dissyllable occurs in
some lines:

> Since—show me where's the woman won without
> The help of this one lie which she believes—
> That—never mind how things have come to pass,
> And let who loves have loved a thousand times—
> All the same he now loves her only, loves
> Her ever! if you "won" you just mean "sold,"
> That's quite another compact.
> (*Inn Album* 2.498-504)

In many cases where Browning's verse is rough, feeble, or prosaic the cause is either the conflict between the prose rhythm and the metrical pattern or the hesitant, scabrous nature of a series of monosyllabic words.

We have seen how the most modest of variations which are common to all iambic pentameter verse and used by all the poets become conspicuous in Browning's poetry because of their frequent and sometimes excessive repetition. We will next look at the different types of lines which he admits into verse whose metrical pattern is iambic pentameter.

CHAPTER V

VARIATIONS IN BLANK VERSE

IN A POEM of blank verse the ear expects to find a metrical pattern made up of ten syllables, divided into five measures by the accent falling on the even ones. This pattern is brought out in some lines with mathematical correctness, as,

He | could not | think he | saw his | wife a | gain:
(Balaustion 2336*)*

The ear becomes patterned to this movement and reaches forward to it with the expectation of finding confirmation in each measure and each line. If a given combination of syllables does not conform exactly to this pattern of anticipation, there is within it an element of surprise, of disappointment or delight. If the natural or prose arrangement of the syllables always coincided with this metrical pattern, there would be intolerable monotony—like little Mary saying her piece. The poets have always prevented this monotony by introducing into the verse some variant element. As a result of long precedent, therefore, certain departures from the "normal" arrangement of syllables have come to be recognized as a part of the rules of verse. They are so common, so universally a part of blank verse, that they hardly need to be mentioned.

1—There may be more than ten syllables. (Usually but one more, though in Browning there may be five more). The extra syllable may be at either end,[1] or within the line.

[1] It is unusual to find them at both ends of the same line:
I' the | crucible of life, where to the | pow*er*s (Prince H. 1322).

(1) At the beginning, or double anacrusis:

Like a | mountain | berry: | doubtless | it is | sweet (*Pauline* 197)

(2) Within the line, or a triple measure:

Scarce | *worth a moth's* | flitting, | which long | grasses | cross,
(*Pauline* 173)

Like the | bright | *side of a* | sorrow, | and the | banks (*Ibid* 60)

(3) At the end, or a feminine ending:

All | I have | clearly | gained; for | once ex- | clud*ing* (*Ibid* 16)

I | cannot | *keep on the* | stretch: 'tis | no back- | shrink*ing*—
(*Ibid* 58)

2—The metrical stress may fall on a syllable which
would not be stressed in a "prose" reading. This light
or failing stress is one of the commonest variations in
poetry, and may occur in any measure:

1st—As | *in* a | Northern | night one |looks al | way
(*Pau.* 48)

2nd—Yet, | suntread | *er,* all | hail!   From | my heart's |
heart   (*Pau.* 201)

3rd—As | we stood | listening | *on* a ¦ sunny | mound
(*Ibid* 65)

4th—Wast | thou to | me, and ¦ art thou | *to* the | world!
(*Ibid* 190)

5th—The | grin with | which I | viewed his | perish | *ing*:
(*Ibid* 119)

There may also be two in the line, as:

Or | with them | *as* an | earnest | *of* their | truth: (*Ibid* 31)

At the | Strozzi, | *at* the | Pillar, | *at* the | Bridge;
(*R&B* 1.110)

There may occasionally be three:

Of | femi | *nine* de | *sira* | bili | *ty*   (*Inn A.* 2.205)

His | tori | *cal* and | *philo* | sophi | *cal* (*Red C. N. C. C.* 3.762)

3—The line may begin with direct attack, or a triple
first measure without an anacrusis:

| *Nothing but* | sky appears, so close the roots   (*Pau.* 783)

4—Any measure may be monosyllabic; it is usually followed by a trisyllabic:

1st—And | *I,* | silent and | scared, got down again
(*R&B* 7.448)

2nd—That | tries for | *truth* | truer than |truth itself,
(*R&B* 11.22)

3rd—"Then, swallowed up in | *rage,* | Stephen ex | claimed
(*R&B* 10.71)

4th—At ease, both gay and | grim, like a | *Swiss* | guard
(*R&B* 11.206)

The same effect is made by the fifth measure (especially when it is enjambed) when it is followed by a direct-attack line:

5th—As if—forgive now—should you let me | sit | Here by the | window with your hand in mine   (*Andrea D. S.* 13-14)

5—The prose phrasing may not coincide with the metrical pattern, resulting in "extra stresses" to bring out the meaning of the line.[2]

Had slammed, jerked, shot, slid,—I shall soon find which!—
(*R&B* 11.222)

Praise, blame, sit, stand, lie or go!—all of it,
(*R&B* 11.616)

Whence, then, this quite new quick cold thrill,—cloudlike,
(*R&B* 10.1248)

Richer than that gold snow Jove rained on Rhodes,
(*R&B* 1.484)

6—A cesura may occur after any syllable in the line to disturb the even movement:

1st—Now,— | never wait the slow envelopment
(*Inn A.* 7.82)

2nd—Would you? | no reason's wanted in the case
(*Ibid* 124)

3rd—So with you! | In they burnt on me, his tales,
(*Ibid* 125)

---

[2] In such cases, the metrical pattern is preserved by aggressive timers by a change in pitch from syllable to syllable.

4th—A life of shame— | I can't distinguish more—
(*Ibid* 133)

5th—Any one told me— | my own mother died
(*Ibid* 119)

6th—He chose to somehow write— | mistakenly
(*Ibid* 109)

7th—Say I have justly judged you! | then farewell
(*Ibid* 102)

8th—Then take love's last and best return! | I think.
(*Ibid* 76)

9th—All sorts of stories of their keeper— | he's
(*Ibid* 76)

And there may be any combination of two or more cesuras in the same line.

When you have listed the foregoing variations, you have all but described the versification of conservative poets, like Milton for instance. But there is nothing very exciting about Milton's prosody; his rules of verse could be written on a card, and after you have listed all his striking variations you have found nothing that is not normal in Robert Browning. In fact, all the things noted in the above list are so mild when set in the perspective of Browning's verse that they are inconspicuous. One almost forgets to note them as a feature of his prosody.

His blank verse is always straining restlessly at the leash of the pattern, nearly always stretching it to the limit, ofttimes actually breaking away from the restraint. He treats the variations just noted as if they too were a part of the "normal," and adds still other unexpected elements to them; he plays variations on the variations. An ear trained to the cadence of Miltonic or Tennysonian blank verse must be readjusted to find pleasure in the lively movement of Browning's shifting patterns.

Shifting, because his phrases do not always rest comfortably when laid over the metrical pattern. They seem to be prompted and arranged more by the compulsion of the thought to be expressed than by the swing of the metre. One can seldom get far away from his own statement that versification is only "a mere outward crust." Any group of phrases that expresses the thought can be inserted in a line of blank verse. The result is that the phrasing, instead of conforming to and reinforcing the pattern, is often in open conflict with it; striving with success to override the expected movement with a new pattern of its own in prevailingly triple rhythm. In many poems—notably *Half Rome, Tertium Quid,* and the Guido monologues of *The Ring and the Book*—the phrasing throws so many measures in successive lines into triple movement that it is a question whether they should not be called duple-triple five-measure lines instead of iambic pentameter.

This fondness of Browning's for hypercatalectic lines gives to his blank verse one of its most distinctive features. If these were occasional, if there were but one extra syllable in a line, if they were liquids or smooth-flowing vowels, if they were "er's," or "ow's," or "le's," etc., one would formulate rules of elision, and the extra syllables would not be any more conspicuous in Browning than in any other poet. But they are not occasional.

Browning takes no pains to make the syllables elide. He must have been quite unconscious, most of the time, of any formula of elision to justify extra syllables. The majority of them are frankly extra syllables, highly race conscious and stubbornly individual. They make therefore the most important variation from the normal in his blank verse.

Single trisyllabic measures are so commonplace that we may take them for granted and pass on. It will be our purpose to show, in the following chapters, the different types of variations which Browning admits into verse whose expected form is iambic pentameter; and how he freely adds other elements, many of them unusual in themselves, to the variations just listed which have released most poets from any sense of monotony.

CHAPTER VI

VARIATION WITH TWO OR MORE TRI-SYLLABIC MEASURES

[There are twenty-nine types of lines with two or more trisyllabic measures. We will, for convenience, arrange them in the following order: (1) those with triples in the first and second measures, with direct attack, an anacrusis, a double anacrusis; then those with triples in the first and third, first and fourth, etc., through the possible combinations (1-15); (2) lines beginning with a double anacrusis and followed by a triple in each of the measures (16-19); (3) lines with three triple measures in the various combinations (20-28); (4) lines with four triple measures (28).]

As we have already noticed, a single triple measure is not unusual in blank verse, unless it recurs in successive lines as it often does in Browning. Any poet might write,

| Boldest of | hearts that | ever | braved the | sun,
(R&B 1.1385)

But it is a rare occasion indeed in Wordsworth, Byron, Shelley, Keats, Tennyson, when this line does not return immediately to duple rhythm after the first measure. Browning's ear, however, did not demand such a return; instead, he allows the triple movement of the first measure to sweep on into the second, establishing a triple-duple movement which conflicts with the expected iambic norm. It is one of the most frequent variations in his blank verse.[1]

---

[1] We are leaving out of account the variations which are universally recognized in all blankverse, as noted above.

| x^{oo} | x^{oo} | x^o | x^o | x

| *Let's to the* | *Prado and* | make the | most of | time.
> (*How it St.* 115)

Peerless above i' the sky, the pinnacle,—
> (*Prince H-S.* 956)

Seeing, there properly was no judgment-bar,
> (*R&B* 1.152)

What's the vague good o' the world, for which you dare
> (*Blougram* 455)

Lies to the end of the list,—"He picked it up,
> (*Sludge* 109)

Whether 't were better have made you man or brute,
> (*Sludge* 1388)

In the earlier poems, there may be an extra syllable at the end of this line:

Smiling humility, praising much, yet waiv*ing* (*Para.* 1.259)
Spoke of the unfinished Duomo, you remem*ber*;
> (*Luria* 1.123)

I, of a sudden must be; my faults, my fol*lies*,
> (*King V.* 1.45)

2—There may be an anacrusis at the beginning of the line which subdues slightly the abruptness of the first triple:

o | x^{oo} | x^{oo} | x^o | x^o | x

<u>As</u> | *she in the* | *gallery* | where the | pictures | glow:
> (*Balcony* 152)

I said to myself—"I have caught it, I conceive
> (*R&B* 6.1162)

And Prince o' the Power of the Air. Our very flight,
> (*R&B* 6.1794)

The last o' the red o' the rose away, while yet
> (*R&B* 3.871)

And life o' the fat o' the land while life should last.
> (*R&B* 2.420)

Was whisked i' the way of a certain man, who snapped.
> (*R&B* 2.275)

As far i' the way o' the Church as safety seemed,
> (*R&B* 4.400)

"Too deep i' the thick of the struggle, struggle through!
(R&B 6.1371)

As yet to the land o' the Bistones." "Then, look
(Balau. 1097)

Sometimes, in the earlier poems, the line has a feminine ending:

Pre | cision and emphasis—you, beside, are clear*ly*
(Para. 3.167)

3—It is rare for this line to have a double anacrusis. For most poets the extra syllable at the beginning would in itself be enough variation for one line; for in continuous verse it has the same value as a triple in any measure, since it is then actually the completion of the fifth measure of the preceding line. The double anacrusis followed by two triples amounts, therefore, to three triples in a row when the verse is considered in paragraphs instead of separate lines.

oo | x^{oo} | x^{oo} | x^o | x^o | x

<u>Like   the</u> | *skipping   of* | *rabbits   by* | moonlight,— | three
slim | shapes,   (*Fra L.* 59)

If he ruffle a feather, it's "Gently, patiently!
(Sludge 161)

From the terrible patience of God? "All which just means,
(R&B 11.1376)

From the first o' the natural fury, not flung loose
(R&B 5.799)

4—Frequently the dactylic movement of the first measure is halted by an iambic second measure, recovers itself in the third and is again halted in the fourth. There results an acute struggle for supremacy between the dactylic and iambic movement.

| x^{oo} | x o | x^{oo} | x^o | x

| *Foxes have* | holes, and | *fowls o' the* | air their | nests;
(R&B 8.1293)

Guido and Pietro, Pietro and Guido, din   (*R&B* 8.261)
Something-or-other jostled Lex this-and-that.
                                                (*R&B* 1.225)
Slow from the innermost o' the palace, stopped (*Balau.* 665)
Tush! I have said it, did I not say it all? (*Balcony* 850)
"*I've* got a V-note!"—what do you say to him?
                                                (*Sludge* 103)
Out of the lying, softly and surely spun   (*Sludge* 405)
Bold in my own, defying the imbeciles—   (*Sludge* 594)
Having a friend, you see, in the Corner-house!
                                                (*Fra Lippo* 227)
Well, and the common sense o' the world calls you
                                                (*Blougram* 264)
Cleave to the husband, be it for weal or woe:
                                                (*R&B* 5.580)
Such was the pact: Pompilia from the first   (*R&B* 5.605)
Such was the starting; now of the further step.
                                                (*R&B* 5.752)
Half below-ground already indeed. Goodbye!
                                                (*R&B* 5.1455)

5—This line may begin less abruptly with an anacrusis. It is pleasingly balanced between duple and
triple movement, pulling now one way, now the other.

o | x⁰⁰ | x⁰ | x⁰⁰ | x⁰ | x

The | *rest o' the* | scheme would | *care for it* | self: es | cape
                                                (*R&B* 11.1613)
Forgotten or misdelivered, and let it work:
                                    (*Death in D.* 167) & (332)
As copy and quote the infamy chalked broad
                                                (*Blougram* 965)
Accomplices in rascality: this we hear   (*Sludge* 373)
Saint Somebody Else, his Miracles, Death and Life,—
                                                (*R&B* 1.80)
Amends for the past, release for the future! Such
                                                (*R&B* 4.1267)
And best o' the stock! Pompilia, thine the palm!
                                                (*R&B* 9.1302)
No more, and the Camp as little, the ingrates,—come,
                                                (*R&B* 5.404)

And robbing a man, but . . . *Excellency*, by your leave,
                              (*R&B* 4.257)
And this you admire, you men o' the world, my lords?
                              (*R&B* 5.554)

6—There may also be a double anacrusis. When this occurs, the line is pulled still farther away from the iambic pattern, because the sensation of a triple measure is carried into the line from the preceding one.

$$\text{oo} \mid \text{x}^{\text{oo}} \mid \text{x}^{\text{o}} \mid \text{x}^{\text{oo}} \mid \text{x}^{\text{o}} \mid \text{x}$$

Is the | *cunning and* | impu | *dence o' the* | pair of | cheats,
                              (*R&B* 5.1493)
At the broidery-frame alone i' the chamber,—loud
                              (*R&B* 7.479)
O' the head of Pietro and Violante—(still
                              (*R&B* 9.805)
And the luck o' the first discovery fell, beside,
                              (*R&B* 4.551)
I' the name of the indivisible Trinity!   (*R&B* 5.121)

7—Again, the triple movement of the first measure, halted by duples in the second and third, may reappear in the fourth. The line limps along between the two movements, with a jump at the beginning and a hop at the end.

$$\mid \text{x}^{\text{oo}} \mid \text{x}^{\text{o}} \mid \text{x}^{\text{o}} \mid \text{x}^{\text{oo}} \mid \text{x}$$

| *Stopped by a* | conch a | top from | *fluttering* | forth
—Sowing the Square with works of one and the same
                              (*R&B* 1.66-67)
Even the blind can see a providence here.   (*R&B* 2.86)
Anxious to learn, of any way i' the world,   (*R&B* 5.430)
Down to that choice example Aelian gives   (*R&B* 1.229)

In the earlier poems, there may be a feminine ending.

You were the last to keep the ford i' the val*ley*
                              (*Luria* 2.137)

8—The line may begin with an anacrusis:

$$\text{o} \mid \text{x}^{\text{oo}} \mid \text{x}^{\text{o}} \mid \text{x}^{\text{o}} \mid \text{x}^{\text{oo}} \mid \text{x}$$

As | *rogues at a* | fair some | fool they | *strip i' the* | midst,
                              (*R&B* 5.1489)

A little at this Lorenzo. Body o' me!   (*R&B* 2.100)
And usual faces,—fain would settle himself (*R&B* 3.291)
Pompilia penned him letters, passionate prayers,
(*R&B* 3.897)
A conjurer? Choose me any craft i' the world
(*Sludge* 437)
Perforce o' the little to succeed i' the large,
(*Inn A.* 2.317)
Another consideration: have it your way!   (*R&B* 4.1189)
Since means to the end are lawful! What i' the way
(*R&B* 9.673)
For*gotten in a* month; or never, or now, revenge!
(*R&B* 4.1523)

9—A double anacrusis is rare.

$$oo \mid x^{oo} \mid x^{o} \mid x^{o} \mid x^{oo} \mid x$$

O' the | *Power o' the* | Air, in | to a | *Heaven: there* | is
(*Inn A.* 4.455)
Violante, triumphing in a flourish of fire   (*R&B* 4.193)
In the eye o' the world? They brandish law 'gainst law;
(*R&B* 4.632)

10—Again, the first and fourth measures may be duple, the second and third triple. The line then begins and ends in the expected movement, but the middle pulls it apart. It usually has an anacrusis.

$$o \mid x^{o} \mid x^{oo} \mid x^{oo} \mid x^{o} \mid x$$

A | simple | *friar o' the* |*city; con* | fessed to | him,
(*R&B* 3.1013)
Which else would heavily fall. On the other hand,
(*R&B* 3.1383)
'Tis but a foot in the water and out again; (*Sludge* 198)
Behaved unpleasantly, till he was fain confess,
(*Sludge* 551)
And wealth to you for a rise i' the world thereby."
(*R&B* 4.516)
I do say, full i' the face o' the crucifix   (*R&B* 11.605)
Amid the general brown o' the species, lurks (*R&B* 4.342)
Would not you prophesy—"She on whose brow is stamped
(*R&B* 5.882)

11—A double anacrusis is a very great rarity.

oo | x⁰ | x⁰⁰ | x⁰⁰ | x⁰ | x

To es | cape the | *questioning* | *guard at the* | proper | gate,
(*R&B* 1.197)

12—There may be a triple in the second and fourth measures. The alteration emphasizes the conflict between the two movements for supremacy. It always has an anacrusis.

o | x⁰ | x⁰⁰ | x⁰ | x⁰⁰ | x

De | duction | *to it,"* *We* | struggle, | *fain to en* | large
(*Cleon* 245)
To spy a providence in the fire's going out, (*Sludge* 962)
Then, since a trial ensued, a touch o' the same
(*R&B* 1.1097)
Be cautious, though: at the *Ave!* "You of the court!
(*R&B* 6.649)
My house, to hustle and edge me out o' the same,
(*R&B* 4.595)
To go with the dowry, and be followed in time
(*R&B* 4.334)
And so Pompilia,—as the move o' the maw, (*R&B* 9.451)
Each playing prodigal son of heavenly sire, (*R&B* 11.757)
Its rules are idiot's-rambling. Honor of birth,—
(*R&B* 5.437)

13—A double anacrusis with this line is very rare.

oo | x⁰ | x⁰⁰ | x⁰ | x⁰⁰ | x

Is a | threat,—whose | *remedy* | of Pom | *pilia's* | wrong,
(*R&B* 10.974)
I' the matrimonial thrust and parry, at least (*R&B* 4.547)

14—The first and second may be duple, the third and fourth triple. The last half of the line runs away with the expected pattern,

o | x⁰ | x⁰ | x⁰⁰ | x⁰⁰ | x

And | carried | by the |*Prince o' the* | *Power of the* | Air
(*R&B* 1.561)

Nor prejudice the Prince o' the Power of the air,
> (*R&B* 1.591)

The worship of that prince o' the power o' the air
> (*Prince H.* 2120)

Bravado with submissiveness, prettily fool   (*R&B* 2.76)

But use your sense first, see if the miscreant proved,
> (*R&B* 3.1350)

"The fellow lurking there i' the black o' the box
> (*R&B* 6.410)

15—A double anacrusis rarely occurs.

oo | xo | xo | xoo | xoo | x

By a | witness | to his | *feat i' the* | *following* | age,—
> (*R&B* 5.1496)

There are no more combinations possible to two tri-syllabic measures; but the limit is set by mathematics and not by any rules of prosody.

The double anacrusis is, as we have noted, a mild variation from the normal pattern. Shelley, for example, is fond of it; but in his verse it seldom adds an extra syllable to the line, since it is usually followed by a monosyllabic measure, as,

And the | *wild* | ante | lope, that | starts when | e'er
> (*Alastor* 103)

Browning more often adds an extra syllable to the line, making it a true double anacrusis followed by normal duple measures, as,

Do you | see the | plan de | licious | ly com | plete? (*R&B* 3.1230)

In addition to this, he allows a triple in any measure of the line. In continuous verse this combination has the same effect as two triples, which, in fact, it is. Note, for example the following paragraph:

Pompilia, I supposed their daughter, drew
Breath first 'mid Rome's worst rankness, through the | *deed*
Of a | *drab and a* | *rogue,* was by-blow bastard-*babe*
Of a nameless strumpet, passed off, palmed on *me*
As the daughter with the dowry. Daughter? *Dirt*
O' the kennel!
> (*R&B* 5.766-771)

16—The first may be trisyllabic. It is very frequent.

oo | xoo | xo | xo | xo | x

And split its toe-webs, and now pens the *drudge*
In a | hole o' the | rock and | calls him | Cali | ban;
                    (*Caliban* 165-6)
That man would choose to see the whole world *roll*
I' the slime o' the slough, so he might touch the tip
                    (*Sludge* 768-9)
        See, here's my elbow's *mark*
I' the dust o' the sill. Oh, shut the lattice, pray!
                    (*Pippa* 1.35-6)
Tickling men's ears—the *sect for a quarter of an hour*
I' the teeth of the world which, clown-like, loves to chew
                    (*R&B* 1.305-6)

In the earlier poems a feminine ending may be added:

And again where the cloak hangs, yonder in the sh*ad*ow.
                    (*Luria* 1.126)

17—The second may be trisyllabic.

oo | xo | xoo | xo | xo | x

I' the | blind old | *palace, a |* pitfall | at each | step,
                    (*R&B* 4.1069)
For the part he played: they have summoned him indeed:
                    (*R&B* 4.1459)
To his mind like San Giovanni—"There's the fold,
                    (*R&B* 7.260)
With the unblamed Aethiop,—Hercules spun wool
                    (*R&B* 9.980)
At the Mouth-of-Truth o' the river-side, you know:
                    (*R&B* 11.186)
With a raven feather, and next week found myself
                    (*Sludge* 268)
Of the outworn umbre and bistre! Yet I think
                    (*Sludge* 772)
O' the commonality—whom, unless you prick
                    (*Aris. A.* 3098)
I' the heart and soul o' the taker, so transmutes
                    (*Balau.* 2421)

18—The third may be trisyllabic.

oo | xo | xo | xoo | xo | x

To the | new pro | fession: | *sin o' the |* sly, hence | forth!
                    (*R&B* 11.1992)

To anticipate a little the tardy pack,   (*R&B* 8.1382)
Than the very wounds that follow. Beside the tale
                                    (*R&B* 4.636)
With the other tale, superlative purity   (*R&B* 4.1035)
I' the secret,—his particular ghost, in fine?   (*Sludge* 865)
From the zenith, each the other, her need of him,
                                    (*R&B* 3.1042)
O' the youthful, earnest, passionate—genius, beauty,
                                    (*Sludge* 1424)
O' the kennel! Dowry? Dust o' the street! Naught more,
                                    (*R&B* 5.771)

19—The fourth may be trisyllabic.

$$\text{oo} \mid \text{x}^{\text{o}} \mid \text{x}^{\text{o}} \mid \text{x}^{\text{o}} \mid \text{x}^{\text{oo}} \mid \text{x}$$

Of the | outside | air, the | inside | *weight o' the* | world
                                    (*R&B* 6.935)
Even Paul's astuteness sniffed no harm i' the world.
                                    (*R&B* 3.1511)
By another vile one: her ostensible work   (*R&B* 4.168)
To the least adroit and self-possessed o' the pair.
                                    (*R&B* 4.552)
O' the wane at least, in all things: what do you say
                                    (*R&B* 11.996)
I have told you this whole story over again.
                                    (*R&B* 6.1596)

We have already seen how the fifth becomes tri-syllabic when carried on into a line beginning with a double anacrusis; and again we have reached the mathematical limit of possible combinations.

20—If two triples in a line make war on the duple movement, three of them annihilate it and set up a new movement in its stead. But Browning, caught in the swing of the triple movement, carries it (or it carries him) breathlessly on through three measures.

$$\mid \text{x}^{\text{oo}} \mid \text{x}^{\text{oo}} \mid \text{x}^{\text{oo}} \mid \text{x}^{\text{o}} \mid \text{x}$$

| *Lily-like* | *out o' the* | *cleft i' the* | sun-smit | rock.
                                    (*R&B* 4.322)

He was at Via Vittoria in three skips: (*Ibid* 474)
What is it all to the facts o' the couple's case,   (*Ibid* 642)
What an elaborate theory have we here,   (*Ibid* 854)
Mater—how well the Ovidian distich suits!—
    (*R&B* 9.1354)
Oh, my superiors, oh, the Archbishop's self!
    (*R&B* 10.1476)
Haman! Ahithophel! Gentlemen of the North,
    (*Straf.* 1. 1.90)
Signing himself with the other because of Christ
    (*Fra L.* 155)
Vaulted too loftily over what barred him late,
    (*R&B* 2.1521)
Dragon and devil. His brother Girolamo   (*R&B* 2.487)
Justify that in its place; I am now to say,   (*R&B* 5.781)

21—There may be an anacrusis.

O | x⁰⁰ | x⁰⁰ | x⁰⁰ | x⁰ |x

Or | *what do you* | *say to a* | *touch of the* | devil's | worst?
    (*R&B* 3.944)
But in the idea, the spiritual display,   (*R&B* 8.384)
And favoritism unfashionable: the Pope (*R&B* 3.1470)
As only a "medium," only the kind of thing
    (*Sludge* 612)
Pompilia tires o' the tattle, and shall to bed:
    (*R&B* 7.242)
To brother Abate, who bustled, did his best,
    (*R&B* 4.1296)
This being a fatherly pat o' the cheek, no more.
    (*R&B* 4.1254)
Francesca Vittoria Pompilia and the rest (*R&B* 4.213)

22—The double anacrusis is very unusual, since it then makes a fourteen-syllable line and that is rare even in Browning's verse. There is at least one, and being a run-on line it actually makes four trisyllabic measures in a row. The iambic pattern is, of course, slaughtered.

OO | x⁰⁰ | x⁰⁰ | x⁰⁰ | x⁰ | x

Why not have *taken the* butcher's son, the *boy*
O' the | *baker or* | *candlestick-* | *maker?* *In* | all the | rest,
    (*R&B* 4.589-90)

23—The second measure may be duple, the first, third, and fourth triple. The lone duple barely halts the rush for an instant before it is overpowered by the strong trisyllabic swing of the "o' the's" and "i' the's" or equally effective phrases which press the pattern out of shape.

| x^{oo} | x^o | x^{oo} | x^{oo} | x

| *Fain would be* | down with | *them i' the* | *thick o' the* | filth,
(*Sludge* 397)

Tickling men's ears—the sect for a quarter of an hour
(*R&B* 1.305)

Satan jaunts forth with, shabby and serviceable,
(*R&B* 4.1016)

Follows as he best can, overtakes i' the end.
(*Ibid* 1171)

And, to the tree, said. . . either the spirit o' the fig,
(*R&B* 7.818)

Tasting some richness caked i' the core o' the tree,—
(*Balaus.* 1876)

Whether a change were wrought i' the shows o' the world,
(*D in D* 466)

Leave him to me. Count Guido and brother of mine,
(*R&B* 5.398)

Coiled with a leer at foot of it. There was the end!
(*R&B* 5.1652)

24—It rarely has an anacrusis.

o | x^{oo} | x^o | x^{oo} | x^{oo} | x

No! | *Burying* | nose deep | *down i' the* | *briery* | bush,
(*R&B* 8.300)

I, being of will and power to help, i' the main,
(*Prince H* 1058)

You dreaded the crown, succumbed to the popular cry,
(*R&B* 5.1844)

The double anacrusis, fourteen-syllable line, does not, I think, occur in this combination.

25—The third may be duple, the first, second, and fourth triple, reversing the line by putting the rush at the beginning with the temporary halt toward the end.

| x^{oo} | x^{oo} |→x^{o} | x^{oo} | x

| *Martyr and* | *miracle!"* | quoth the | *other to* | match:

(*R&B* 1.205)

"Now for the Trial!" they roar: "the Trial to test

(*R&B* 4.12)

Aim on my part i' the marriage,—money to-wit. *(Ibid* 611)

Wager-by-battle-of-cheating! What do you say, *(Ibid* 628)

Throw in abuse o' the man, his body and soul, *(Ibid* 726)

Guido rejoins—"Did the other end o' the tale *(Ibid* 1054)

Turns on the pettier, makes a general prey.   *(Ibid* 1565)

Here he has Cardinal This to vouch for the past,

(Ibid 1599)

26—The anacrusis is rare.

o | x^{oo} | x^{oo} | x^{o} | x^{oo} | x

Poor | *glorious* | *spirit—con* | cerns him | *even to* | stay

(*Parac.* 5.15)

My profit or loss i' the matter: married am I:

(*R&B* 5.566)

The double anacrusis, to my knowledge, does not occur.

27—The first measure may be duple, the second, third and fourth triple. It sets up for the nonce a new triple pattern.

o | x^{o} | x^{oo} | x^{oo} | x^{oo} | x

In | keeping | *out o' the* | *way o' the* | *wheels o' the* | world,

(*R&B* 2.664)

Through that irregular breach o' the boundary,—see

(*R&B* 10.1201)

That raised the spirit and succubus,—letters, to-wit,

(*R&B* 5.1132)

28—This line has a double anacrusis, with a feminine ending, and is the most elephantine line in Browning's poetry. It must be considered in its own habitat to be appreciated properly. Incidentally it is a remarkable study in triple rythm in blank verse.

oo | x^{o} | x^{oo} | x^{oo} | x^{oo} | x^{o}

How does it suit the dread tra*ditional test*

O' the | "Great and | *Terrible* | *Name*"?   Shall the | *Heaven*

of | Heavens

Stoop to such child's play?

(*Sludge* 1073-5)

Once again we have reached the limit of possible combinations.

29—Four triples in a line are extremely rare. Since the few examples that occur contain vowels which are considered under the fiction of elision, it is quite possible that Browning intended them to be run together. Explain them any way you please, the sensation of the extra syllables is still with you; but they do not stand out hard and obstreperous as many of his extra syllables do.

$$o \mid x^{oo} \mid x^{oo} \mid x^{oo} \mid x^{oo} \mid x$$

By | *comers and* | *goers in* | *Via Vit* | *toria:* | eh?

(*R&B* 3.74)

The aim o' the cruelty being so crueller still,

(*R&B* 4.684)

CHAPTER VII

BLANK VERSE LINES WITH ONLY FOUR MEASURES

ANOTHER LARGE group of lines raises the question: Does Browning admit four-measure lines into a society of pentameters?

One type of four-measure line has long been a part of pentameter verse—the so-called "heroic tetrameter."[1] It is largely a matter of reading rather than the deliberate design of the poet; and it is, in theory at least, a five-measure line. Its peculiarity consists in the fact that although it contains ten syllables and may be read as a pentameter, it is, as a matter of fact, normally read as a tetrameter without disturbing the ear. It falls naturally into four measures in the reading because the third stress, finding the sixth syllable too weak to bear its burden, is moved on to the eighth and the four syllables between are huddled together into a quadruple measure of approximately the same time value as the other measures. If this weak sixth syllable is flanked by two easily elided ones, as " . . . *er of the*," the tetrameter reading is all but inevitable. Let the reader observe carefully his own reading of these lines:

Threatening the torpor of the inside nose (*Blougram* 671)
Holding the candle to the Sacrament,   (*Fra L.* 118)
Stung by the splendor of a sudden thought, (*Death D.* 59)
Flat on his belly in the pit's much mire,   (*Caliban* 2)
To the breathless fellow at the altar-foot, (*Fra L.* 149)

[1] The peculiarity of this line was recognized and set forth by C. W. Cobb in "A Type of Four-Stress Verse in Shakespeare," *New Shakespeareana* 10:1; "A Scientific Basis for Metrics", *Modern Language Notes*, May, 1913; "A Further Study of the Heroic Tetrameter," *Modern Philology*, 1916; it is interestingly set forth also in C. E. Andrews, *The Writing and Reading of Verse*, pp. 177-182.

Lines of this type have been in pentameter verse for
so long that they are a recognized member of the family; but in theory they are, one may insist, five-measure lines, since the reader may not improperly accent
the sixth syllable strongly enough to mark off a fifth
time division.

Browning has used this heroic tetrameter with great
frequency. And if we may take his practice of writing "o' the" and "i' the" to indicate his own reading
of his lines,[2] we can find unmistakable evidence that
he actually read some of them at least as tetrameter.
For he has sometimes inserted an apostrophe in the
sixth syllable, making it impossible to read the line in
five measures. The indication is that he himself
huddled the third measure with the second and tried
to indicate his reading by using the apostrophe instead
of the consonant. One cannot very well read these
lines as pentameter:

'Thinketh, He dwelleth i' the cold o' the moon.
                              (*Caliban* 25)
Followed her parents i' the face o' the world,
                              (*R&B* 3.720)
Show them, when done with, i' the shape of a child.
                              (*R&B* 3.152)
Goes o'er the gamut o' the creditor's cry (*R&B* 4.137)
But flirting flag-like i' the face o' the world
                              (*R&B* 3.888)
As the other herd quenched, i' the wash o' the wave,
                              (*R&B* 10.846)
Snug-cornered somewhere i' the Basilicate, (*Cenci.* 97)
One sees the pulpit o' the epistle-side, (*Tomb St. P.* 21)
An appariation i' the midst? The rout (*Sord.* 5.127)

These lines are pretty clear instances of "heroic
tetrameter" read, if not deliberately designed, in four

[2] See Chapter IV.

measures. And the margin of difference is hardly pal-
pable between them and a multitude of lines of this
type:

>Having put poison in the posset-cup,   (*R&B* 2.706)
>By this defection of the foolish pair,   (*R&B* 2.524)
>Where the repayment of the servitude   (*R&B* 4.420)
>Sprung from the bowels of the generous steer,
>   (*R&B* 9.1340)
>I' the school, i' the cloister, in the diocese
>   (*R&B* 10.385)

or the balanced phrases so familiar in Pope:

>I hold to the letter and obey the bond (*Prince H. S.* 1470)
>Back to the husband and the house she fled: (*R&B* 2.874)
>The easy husband and the shrewder wife   (*R&B* 4.453)
>To miss the advantage of the golden mean, (*R&B* 4.1270)

Although this type of four-measure line pleases the
ear as a rhythmic variation without seeming to affect
the expected pentameter pattern, any other four-measure type is unusual, startling, and often disturbing.
For these reasons if for no other they are rare or non-
existent. But there are few exclusion bills in Browning's blank verse, and he has admitted some lines which
even the melting pot of aggressive timing leaves un-
assimilated. It does not seem likely that Browning
consciously and deliberately intended them to be in
four measures; by a "super-aggressive" timing while
composing them, he may have forced them into theoretical conformity to his pattern. What has hap-
pened is that the natural order of the prose phrases
has a rhythm quite unlike the expected pattern and
in mortal conflict with it. This rhythm is so strong,
and so inherent in the structure of the phrases as
speech units, that it overrides the metrical pattern of
the verse and sets up a new one of its own. It is always difficult and sometimes impossible to impose the

metrical pattern upon such conflicting prose phrases. In every case, the result is unsatisfactory and the lines are even worse as pentameter than as tetrameter. Any reader, therefore, who comes upon them with an ear not primarily interested in metrics will let the prose rhythm override the pattern and read them in four measures.

Thus, the following line might best be read:

| Did   condemn | Stephen,   a | nathema | tize

(*R&B* 10.134)

The only possibilities of making five measures of the line are either to violate the pronunciation of "anathematize" by reading:

| Did   condemn | Stephen, | ana | thema | tize

or introduce a monosyllabic measure:

Did con | demn | Stephen, a | nathema | tize

both of which seem unnatural and forced.   So with the lines:

Waiting to see what Delilah dares do!

(*R&B* 11.2195)

Old sores scratch kindly, the ass makes a push

(*R&B* 9.1278)

Flung herself thrice at the Archbishop's feet,

(*R&B* 4.795)

Count Guido once more between heaven and me,

(*R&B* 3.1149)

Ungenerous thrift of each marital debt

(*R&B* 9.1304)

The intrigue, the elopement, the disguise,—well charged!

(*R&B* 6.1706)

And years make men restless—they needs must spy

(*R&B* 3.285)

Unrecognized yet, but perceptible?   (*R&B* 10.1866)

And conquered,—the world never heard the like!

(*R&B* 11.1280)

The space circumjacent, for fit demesne, (*R&B* 11.2151)

And, in a commendable charity   (*R&B* 2.1092)

Was marching in marital rectitude!   (*R&B* 5.857)

And so forth, the poor inexperienced bride,
                                        (*R&B* 2.519)
And only unused to the brotherly look.   (*R&B* 1.1095)

The acknowledgment of, and the penitence for,
                                        (*R&B* 4.1474)
By the look o' the lady,—to dare disobey
                                        (*R&B* 6.997)

These lines are more at home in anapestic tetrameter than in blank verse; they fit into the pattern of Byron's *Farewell to the Muse* without the slightest disturbance:

Can they speak of the friends that I lived but to love? (6.1)
By the look o' the lady,—to dare disobey.
And only unused to the brotherly look.

There is also a group of perplexing lines which seem to have no kinship with their brethren. Any decent pentameter reading is, we think, impossible. But they are pleasing tetrameters, and may perhaps be best read thus:

'Gainst the | blind bull- | front of a | brute-force-| world?
                                        (*Luria* 1.94)
With the | first stone- | slab of the | staircase | cold,
                                        (*R&B* 1.114)
While an | inch out | side where those | blood-bright |
     eyes,   (*R&B* 1.610)
From the | old cold | shade and un | happy | soil
                                        (*R&B* 2.1181)
And the | flesh fails, | now, and the | time is | come,—
                                        (*Straf.* 1.2.103)

where the importance of "bull," "force," "stone," etc., is brought out and the pattern preserved by changes in pitch.

CHAPTER VIII

DIRECT ATTACK WITH DUPLE FIRST MEASURE
(An Unusual Variation)

LINES WITH direct attack in which the first measure is not trisyllabic have not been in favor with the poets since the Elizabethan period. They have always preferred lines of this type:

| *Sleeping a* | bove her | robe as | buoyed by | clouds,

(Cleon 136)

where the anacrusis is, as it were, compensated for by the extra syllable in the first measure.

In Browning's verse the natural prose rhythm of the phrases is sometimes in conflict with the theory of this line, and frequently it is strong enough to overcome the expected movement, when the first phrase is composed of three words, of which the first and third are very emphatic, and is followed by a cesura or an unemphatic syllable. Thus, in the line

| Doomed to | *death, such a* | double | death as | waits

(R&B 3.207)

the first and third syllables are emphatic and must be accented, while the fourth is unemphatic and unaccented. The phrasing, therefore, overrides the expected pattern for direct-attack lines by making the first measure duple and the second triple.

The resultant line only lacks a feminine ending to be a perfect example of the classical hendecasyllabic, whose pattern was

$$| \; x^o \; | \; x^{oo} \; | \; x^o \; | \; x^o \; | \; x^o$$

In the early poems where Browning made full use of

the feminine ending, the final syllable is often supplied and the lines are good hendecasyllables.

| Light for | *me in the* | darkness | tempering | sorrow
(*Para.* 5.72)

This,—lest you even more than needs, embitter
(*Soul's Tr.* 1.22)

Men take pains to preserve a tree stump, even,
(*Ibid.* 1.202)

It may be merely an accident of phrasing, or it may well be the direct influence of the classical hendeca-syllabic which throws so many of Browning's pentameter lines into this or related patterns. Several recognizable types keep recurring through the blank verse.

1—Beginning with direct attack, the first may be duple, the second triple, the rest duple. It is everywhere in Browning, being only a little less frequent than direct-attack lines with two trisyllabic measures.

| x⁰ | x⁰⁰ | x⁰ | x⁰ | x

| Bid the | *few, better* | favored | in the | brain,
(*Prince H-S* 1493)

Root and branch, with much roaring, and some blood,
(*Ibid* 1563)

Mu and *Epsilon* stand for my own name.
(*Death in D.* 9)

—So to speak—in a certain sort—his wife.
(*R&B* 1.198)

Doomed to death, such a double death as waits
(*R&B* 3.207)

That's the way to write Latin, friend my Fisc!
(*R&B* 8.196)

I am he that aspired to *know*: and thou?
(*Paracelsus* 2.384)

Not so large as this noisy Rome, no doubt, (*R&B* 7.562)

He's at home, only acts by proxy here: (*R&B* 4.651)

Thanks to whom? When the mother speaks the word,
(*R&B* 11.1047)

2—The first type is not absent from other poets; it seems to be an accident of phrasing which upsets the regular movement. Sometimes the phrasing is strong enough to defy the iambic movement until the third measure, where a triple may halt the strong trochaic movement.

| x^o | x^o | x^{oo} | x^o | x
| Free as | unborn | *babe from con* | nivance | at
(R&B 8.893)

Since the whole need not the physician! Brief,
(R&B 9.1211)

Let me look at thee in the flesh as erst, (<i>R&B</i> 10.1004)

"All which work takes time: till to-morrow, then,
(Ibid 2108)

One makes fools look foolisher fifty-fold (<i>R&B</i> 11.850)

John, who made things Boehme wrote thoughts about?
(Transc. 38)

Men are men: why then need I say one word
(R&B 3.877)

There I lay, then, all my great fortnight long,
(R&B 7.1670)

Other lines may or may not fall into the pattern according to the reading; they may be forced into a normal pattern.

None of this vile way by the barren words
(R&B 10.348)

Then, if I got safe to my place again,
(R&B 11.1816)

"Rub all out!" Well, well, there's my life, in short,
(Fra L. 221)

Here, though all else changed in the changing world!
(R&B 7.1402)

3—There are a few lines in which the phrasing is so hostile to the normal pattern that they seem to be trochaic up to the fourth measure. Other readings are possible, but, I think, even less satisfactory.

| x^o | x^o | x^o | x^{oo} | x
| What care | I,—by | God's gloved | *hand or the* | bare?
(R&B 10.1402)

Five years long, now, rounds faith into my ears,
                              (*R&B* 10.1584)
Means were found, plan laid, time fixed, she avers
                              (*R&B* 3.915)
Is your charge to stay with me till I die? (*R&B* 11.136)

4—Two triples are rare in this already unusual line, but they may occur in the second and third in an evenly balanced line:

$$| x^o \quad | x^{oo} | x^{oo} | x^o \quad | x$$

| Tried, all | *five, and found* | *guilty and* | put to | death
                              (*R&B* 1.123)
Should quite starve while Authority sat at meat;
                              (*R&B* 9.1104)
Sweet and clean, dining daintily, dizened smart,
                              (*Sludge* 269)
How it rained!—through our street and the Lion's-
    mouth   (*R&B* 7.423)
'Sir,' said she, and so following. "Why more words?
                              (*R&B* 9.934)

5—Or there may be a triple in the second and fourth, causing the line to gallop between two movements.

$$| x^o | x^{oo} | x^o \quad | x^{oo} | x$$

| Thou, not | *Pope but the* | mere old | *man o' the* | world,
                              (*R&B* 10.392)
Hence a plan for so plaguing, body and soul,
                              (*R&B* 10.601)
Paul steps back the due distance, clear o' the trap
                              (*R&B* 10.889)

6—The phrasing is never quite strongly trochaic enough to pull the line into the other possible combination of two trochees and two dactyls, which such lines as the following tend to do:

| Holds   a   germ— | sand-grain | weight   too | much   i'
    the | scale—   (*R&B* 3.140)

CHAPTER IX

THE MONOSYLLABIC MEASURES

ALL POETS have used, as variations from the expected verse pattern, monosyllabic measures, usually followed by a trisyllabic measure as a theoretical "compensation" for the catalexis. This variation has become so familiar to English readers through the constant use of the poets that, like direct attack or a triple measure, it delights the ear without very greatly surprising it. But the poets have, in general, been so uniform in their practice that this variation has come to have a fixed form of its own, or a relief pattern in the larger figure of the verse. Usage has fixed a certain form for each measure in the line, and our ears have learned to expect that if the poet chooses to vary the normal pattern by introducing a monosyllabic measure, he will follow the custom and write:

(1) And | I,^ | silent and | scared, got | down a | gain
                (*R&B* 7.448)

(2) Make | both ends | meet—^ | nothing the | vulgar
    loves   (*R&B* 2.513)

(3) With | leave to | clench the | past^, | chain the to- |
    come,   (*Balcony* 64)

(4) To | weep de | caying | wits ere the | frail^ | body
                (*Paul.* 553)

A line with a monosyllabic measure has already departed considerably from the normal pattern and has satisfied most poets' desire for variation and relief. If then there be added to this already varied line still other variations, our expectancy is teased still further and we experience surprise (agreeable or offensive according to the reader) as we try to assimilate the

unusual elements into the normal pattern. It is precisely these unexpected elements added to an already
unusual line, that makes Browning's lines so striking
and metrically interesting.

A monosyllable is most conspicuous in the first and
in the fourth measure; prominent and more frequent
but less conspicuous in the second and third. In the
first measure its usual form among all poets is

> And | I,ᴬ | silent and | scared, got down again

A double anacrusis or a feminine ending add but little:

> *In the* | new ᴬ | order of | things,—he | plays the | priest;
> (*R&B* 10.1905)
> Them | selves ᴬ | fair and for | gotten; | yes, for | got*ten*
> (*Para.* 4.208)

But if the triple measure is delayed, as,

> A | priest—ᴬ | what else | *should the con* | soler | be?
> (*R&B* 2.776)
> O' the | red ᴬ | thread through | *that insig* | nifi | cance!
> (*R&B* 11.2068)
> When the | wide ᴬ | town's his | hen-roost! | *Fie o' the* | fool!"
> (*R&B* 2.832)

or absent, as,

> "And the | fireᴬ | shuts out | me and | shuts in | you!
> (*R&B* 4.840)
> Getting | dry,ᴬ | sweet and | proper | for next | week,—
> (*R&B* 11.208)
> And the | house,ᴬ | late dis | tracted | by their | peals,
> (*R&B* 2.686)

we get a typical Browning line full of unexpected
elements.

The unexpected element may also be an extra triple
in the line,

> My | wifeᴬ | *fled in the* | *company* | of a | priest, (*R&B* 3.824)
> There | lie,ᴬ | *sullen me* | *morial* | and no | more (*Para.* 2.7)
> The | tract,ᴬ | *doomed to per* | *petual* | barren | ness,
> (*Para.* 2.116)

At the | town's^ | *edge by a* | *gate i' the* | Pauline | Way,
(*R&B* 5.1330)
Oh, the | wife ^ | *knew the ap* | *propriate* | warfare | well,
(*R&B* 2.859)

Or it may be the absence of an anacrusis, a rare but striking form occurring in the dramas.

| Pym?^ | Pym and the | People. | Oh, the | Faction!
(*Straf.* 1.2.62)
| Great?^ | let it be | great; but the | joys it | brought,
(*Pippa* 1.162)

And I drew
| Back;^ | put far | back your | face with | both my | hands
(*Pippa* 1.172)

The phrasing of many other lines pulls them towards this same type without ever entirely overcoming the normal pattern, as,

Found,—furnishing a last and best regale,—
(*R&B* 2.1062)
Paul,—finding it moreover past his strength
(*R&B* 5.1346)
—Paul, finally, in such a state of things,
(*R&B* 5.1360)

A monosyllabic fourth measure is also very frequent and equally conspicuous in Browning's verse, as it is in Shelley's. In most instances, though not in all, it is due to the fact that an important adjective, when it follows a light or failing stress, usually attracts the metrical stress to itself, giving lines of this type:

At | ease, both | gay and | grim, like a | Swiss^ | guard
(*R&B* 11.206)
And said, "The old man sleeps with a young^ wife."
(*Pippa* 1.26)
As the Pope's pantoufle does on the Pope's^ foot.
(*R&B* 4.459)
And Saviles! Make your mind up, o' God's^ love,
(*Straf.* 1.2.147)
I mean to meet you on your own^ premise:
(*Bloug.* 171)

" 'Ripe fig, burst skin, regale the fig^-pecker—
$$(R\&B\ 7.825)$$
Reigns paramount i' the world, for the large^ good
$$(Prince\ H\ 1481)$$
Made the avowal easy, the shame^ slight?
$$(R\&B\ 2.587)$$

Lines in which the second measure is monosyllabic occur more frequently, with less surprise, and with more variations than any other.   The reason for its unusual frequency is, without doubt, Browning's preference for the cesura after the fourth or fifth syllable,[1] and an "inverted" measure following immediately after the pause. The expected form, common among all poets, is:

Make | both ends | meet,^— | *nothing the* | vulgar | loves
$$(R\&B\ 2.513)$$
"For such a prank,^ death is the penalty!"
$$(R\&B\ 11.120)$$
I' the mouth of man,^ woman and child—to-wit
$$(R\&B\ 5.618)$$

But Browning introduces into the line other elements which pull against this expected pattern and surprise the reader.

It is common to find the triple measure preceding the monosyllable in an unpleasantly jerky line:

By | *one and the* | same^ | pitchy | furnace | stirred
$$(R\&B\ 10.874)$$
"Or *rather*," *laugh* foes,^ "then did there befall
$$(R\&B\ 4.1337)$$
The *worth of what's* lost,^ sum of damage done.
$$(R\&B\ 2.1501)$$
Foam, *fling myself* flat,^ rend my clothes to shreds;
$$(Sludge\ 306)$$
Soft, *innocent*, warm,^ moist, impassable,
$$(Sludge\ 541)$$

[1] The table compiled by Morton shows this distribution:

1	2	3	4	5	6	7	8	9
7.48	8.85	10.35	17.42	16.39	13.10	13.67	8.94	3.61

Quoth *Paolo once* more,^ "Mothers, wives and maids,
               (*R&B* 4.501)
Is it *settled so* far?^   Settled or disturbed,
               (*R&B* 4.1272)

Or the triple measure may be supplanted by a double anacrusis:

Can she | feel no | love?^ | Let her | show the | more,
               (*R&B* 11.1403)
Oh how right that is,^   how like Jesus Christ
               (*R&B* 7.1812)
"*What the* whole man meant,^ whom you wish you knew,"
               (*Prince H* 60)

A single triple measure following the monosyllable is always expected; but Browning likes to add one or more triples to the line as a further variation. If they both precede and follow the monosyllable, the line is pleasingly balanced:

And | *flower o' the* | field,^ | *all in a* | common | pact
               (*R&B* 10.1074)
The *birth o' the* boy^ *warrant the* bolder crime,
               (*R&B* 4.1099)
In a *case o' the* kind?^ *None, as she* all but says.
               (*R&B* 2.1509)
I' the *regular* way,^ *each at its* proper court,
               (*R&B* 4.1325)
And the *rest o' the* tale?^ *Yet the tale's* true, you know:
               (*Sludge* 983)
But *what if the* whole^ prove a *prank o' the* pen,
               (*R&B* 5.1199)
The *curd o' the* cream,^ *flower o' the wheat, as it* were,
               (*R&B* 1.910)

But if both triples follow, the last measures rush away from the first in triple movement:

On | what came | first,^ | *clothes and a* | *trinket or* | two,
               (*R&B* 3.1069)
And here I sprawl:^ *where is the company?* Gone!
               (*R&B* 11.112)

> And still declare—^*life, without absolute* use
> <div align="right">(<i>R&B</i> 11.1482)</div>
> Or the 'Stars and Stripes'^ *set to consecutive* fourths."
> <div align="right">(<i>Sludge</i> 346)</div>

The practice of the poets has also led us to expect this line to begin with direct attack. Ever since Surrey, readers have been made familiar with this pleasing variant from the normal pattern:

> | *Babes and not* | beasts^— | *beasts and not* | stocks and | stones! |
> <div align="right">(<i>R&B</i> 6.1798)</div>
> | *Just as they* | are,^ | *careless what* | comes of | it?
> <div align="right">(<i>Fra. L.</i> 294)</div>

But Browning treats this line as though it were in itself the normal pattern and adds to it some further variations of his own. He may delay the triple to the fourth measure:

> | *Master of* | men^— | touch one | *hair of the* | five
> <div align="right">(<i>R&B</i> 2.1461)</div>

or he may add a third triple:

> | *Mine shall have* | been,^— | *seeing there's* | ill in the | end
> <div align="right">(<i>R&B</i> 11.1442)</div>
> | *Fools to the* | depth,^ | *fools to the* | level be | tween,
> <div align="right">(<i>R&B</i> 11.1754)</div>

or both triples may follow the monosyllable in an unusual line:

> | This good | God,^— | *what he could* | do, if he | would,
> <div align="right">(<i>Blougram</i> 192)</div>
> | Hands and | feet,^ | *scrambling some* | how, and so | dropped,
> <div align="right">(<i>Fra L.</i> 65)</div>
> | Sham the | worse,^ | *damn herself* | *praiseworthi* | ly!
> <div align="right">(<i>R&B</i> 11.1404)</div>

In another type of interesting variation, the phrasing is able to make a quadruple of one measure:

> | *Jealous that the* | good^ | trick which | served the | turn
> <div align="right">(<i>Prince H</i> 12)</div>
> *Rachel of the* blue^ eye and golden hair,
> <div align="right">(<i>R&B</i> 5.1305)</div>

Clear my head^ *dizzy with the* hubbub—say
(*Imperante* 26)
"Play the man,^ *pity the o*ppressed!"—no pause,
(*R&B* 10.1553)
Yield its like,^ *propagate a* bliss in turn (*R&B* 3.149)
Shine and shade,^ *happiness and* misery (*Bean- S.* 5)
Weaves no web,^ *watches on the* ledge of tombs,
(*Epistle* 46)

Such lines have but little in common with iambic pentameter verse; except to an aggressive timer, they are prose.

There is one other type of line whose phrasing is so opposed to a five-measure iambic line that only by the most vigorous aggressive timing can it be prevented from becoming a six-measure line with a monosyllabic second measure. It is like those just noted, except that the phrasing prevents the syllables from huddling into a quadruple measure. It is one of the most numerous of Browning's variations.

| Fret or | sulk,^ | grin or | whimper, | any | mood
(*Sludge* 602)
Eyes to see,^ ears to hear, and hands to help,
(*Sludge* 829)
—Terni's fall,^ Naples' bay and Gothard's top—
(*Blougram* 533)
Inn that's out^—out of sight and out of mind
(*Inn A.* 1.191)
Aunt and niece,^ you and me. At night arrive;
(*Inn A.* 1.193)
Right for me,^—right for you the fine and fair!
(*Red C.* 44)
Prayers move God;^ threats, and nothing else, move men!
(*R&B* 7.1608)

A very slight shift in the phrasing makes the fourth measure (if the reader agrees that these are best read as six-measure lines), also monosyllabic.

| Filched my | name,^ | hemmed me | round,^ | hustled me
| hard (*R&B* 5.1488)

Lies to God,^ lies to man,^ every way lies (*R&B* 4.216)
Were loud or mute,^ wept or laughed,^ cursed or jeered,
(*R&B* 10.97)

There is very little difference between lines with monosyllabic second measures and those with monosyllabic third measures; the latter is only a little less frequent than the former and has always been in favor among the poets. The usual and expected form of the line is:

With | leave to | clench the | past,^ | *chain the to-* | come,
(*Balcony* 64)

where the cesura is followed by a choriambic phrase. The unexpected elements which Browning adds to this line are, in general, the same as those just noted for lines with the second measure monosyllabic; and they occur in the same general combinations. Thus, the triple often precedes the monosyllable:

Man | pure of | *evil in* | thought,^ | word and | deed—
(*Mihrab S.* 17)
He—"No, thy *Guido is* rough,^ heady, strong,
(*R&B* 10.1456)
A *cannon full*-blown so far;^ priest, and priest
(*R&B* 2.781)

Or the double anacrusis may supplant the triple:

Hunted | forth to | go hide | head,^ | starve and | die,
(*R&B* 10.561)
From a cleft rose-peach the whole^ Dryad sprang.
(*Pippa* 2.92)

Or there may be two or more triples:

The | *hoard i' the* | *heart o' the* | toad,^ | hell's quin | tessence.
(*R&B* 2.1368)
Yet | *leave i' the* | *lurch at the* | first ^| spit of | rain,
(*R&B* 11.740)
| *Money for* | *money,—and* | they,^ | bride for | groom,
(*R&B* 4.522)
| *Gain a con* | *ception of* | what,^— | how and | why, (*Sun* 44)
It | smarts a | *little to* | day,^ | *well in a* | week. (*R&B* 4.1522)

Who | played the | *regular* | game,^— | *priest and A* | bate,
(R&B 4.392)

.The | new e | *pistle from* | Rome.^ | *"All to no* | use!
(R&B 5.1431)

| *Left to walk* | *warily* | now.^ | *how does she* | walk?
(R&B 2.758)

| *Full to the* | *depth o' the* | wick,^— | *money's so* | much;
(R&B 4.76...

| *What shall be* | *mistily* | seen,^ | *murmuringly* | heard,
(R&B 1.751)

| *Though but the* | *chink o' the* | bell,^ | *turn o' the* | hinge
(R&B 3.38)

In the early poems and plays, however, where the feminine ending is common, this line takes on a distinctive form. The distincton is due to the fact that the extra syllable changes the usual choriambic phrase at the end of the line into a pleasing adonic. It sounds like an echo of the short lines in *A Grammarian's Funeral.*

My | portion, | my re | ward,^ | *even my* | *failure,*
(Para. 2.75)

The giant shades of fate,^ *silently flitting,*
(Paul. 570)

His hold; and from the East,^ *fuller and fuller,*
(Para. 3.1036)

The ultimate effect:^ *sooner or later*   (*Para.* 3.920)
From my proud eminence.^ *Fortune is fickle*
(Para. 3.595)

To get him from the fire.^ *Nothing but saying*
(Pippa 1.75)

It is quite unusual, even in Browning, to find two monosyllabic measures in a single line. One type, in which the first and third are monosyllabic, occurs comparatively frequently. It may take this form:

Of | you,^ | me and him | self, | knowing he | lies,
(R&B 10.367)

Why, men^—men and not boys^—boys and not babes—
(R&B 6.1797)

> As I supped,^ ate the coarse bread,^ drank the wine
> > (*R&B* 5.1381)

or the "adjective" form familiar in Tennyson's Idylls:

> On a | stone^ | bench in a | close^ | fetid | cell, (*R&B* 1.1278)
> To the green^ woods in the gay^ summer time.
> > (*Paul.* 369)
> By the dark^ rock and the white^ wave just breaking
> > (*Paul.* 664)
> Till the red^ fire on its glazed^ windows spread
> > (*Pippa* 1.178)

Other types are less common, but they do occur with the first and fourth monosyllabic:

> To the | wind^ | murmuring | in the | damp^ | copse,
> > (*Paul* 66)
> Some vase^ shaped to the curl of the God's^ lip,
> > (*Balcony* 710)
> Ah, the Court!^ yes, I come to the Court's^ self;
> > (*R&B* 5.1158)

And the second and fourth:

> What | mattered the | fierce^ | beard or the | grim^ | face?
> > (*R&B* 7.417)
> Close under the stone^ wall by the south^ entry.
> > (*Pippa* 1.61)

A few lines are pulled strongly, if not irresistibly, into six measures:

> The | red^ | hand is | sworn^ | foe of the | black^ | jaw.
> > (*R&B* 11.434)
> The deep^ groves and white^ temples and wet^ caves:
> > (*Paul.* 332)
> A sad^ thought, a sad^ fate! how very full
> > (*Par.* 5.286)
> The cheek^ burns, the blood^ tingles, when you speak
> > (*Straf.* 4.2.171)
> Filched my name,^ hemmed me round,^ hustled me hard
> > (*R&B* 5.1488)
> Lies to God,^ lies to man,^ every way lies
> > (*R&B* 4.216)

CHAPTER X

ELISION

IT IS POSSIBLE that some poets believed that the pentameter line should not exceed ten syllables, and that redundant syllables could be "elided" and reduced to this ideal number according to certain rules. Spenser, with a syllable theory on his mind, printed elisions thus:

> 'Gainst all the gods, and th' empire sought from them
> to beare."   (*F. Q.* 7.6.1.9)

But even the poets who have held to the theory of elision have not always indicated them in this manner. The rules are, in general, the same as those which Mr. Bridges worked out to explain Milton's redundant lines:

(1) Open vowels may be elided.
(2) Vowels separated by l, n, or r.
(3) E before final n, as in "given," "even," "heaven."
(4) The 2nd person singular of verbs.
(5) Normal speech contractions such as "e'en," "twxt," etc.

It is quite true that many lines can be reduced to a theoretical standard by applying these rules. It is also true that one must elide his imagination to bring some lines from as regular a poet as Milton into harmony with rules of elision. Such a line as

> Of rainbows and starry eyes. The waters thus
>   (*P. L.* 7.446)

will triple in spite of any rule.

But the question is, did Browning hold to the theory of ten syllables? and did he have any rules of elision? The answer to both questions is "No."

Browning had no theory of syllable counting; that is the most obvious truth about his blank verse. As we have already seen, he knew that the number of syllables did not matter so long as the ear was satisfied that the time parts were approximately even. So he wrote pentameters varying in length from nine to fifteen syllables, without violating the temporal equality of the measures. His ear was pleased by triple measures in his duple patterns, and required no fiction of elision to rationalize them. Coleridge had already in *Christabel* justified them on a perfectly sound basis. It is then not only unnecessary but also futile to try to reduce these extra syllables to rules of elision, for two simple reasons. One is that elision is in most cases really nothing but a metrical fiction because the triple effect of the extra syllable cannot be obscured, and because the extra syllable does not affect the temporal equality of the measure in which it occurs. The other is that, for every line in Browning which can be compressed through elision to ten syllables, there are perhaps five or more which will compress under no rules whatever. It is impossible therefore to tell with certainty whether or not he intended elision even in those lines where it is theoretically possible. If all the lines were of this type:

And found *the old* adversa*ry ath*wart the path—
(*R&B* 7.1602)
From glo*ry of* pain to *glory of* joy; and so,
(*R&B* 10.1796)

they could be elided according to rule, and one could suspect Browning of a ten-syllable theory. But he also writes lines of this type:

Like the skipping of rabbits by moonlight,—three slim
shapes,   (*Fra L.* 59)

where no elision is possible.

And even the elision may still leave in the line a redundant syllable:

> She unlatched door, let all the *devils o' the* dark
> (*R&B* 5.1505)
> *I' the* soul, *do you* see—its tense or *tremulous* part—
> (*R&B* 5.30)

The printing does not indicate such easy elisions as this:

> Show cause for what he has done, the irregular deed,
> (*R&B* 5.99)

The only unmistakable elisions in Browning therefore are those normal contractions which he has printed with an omitted letter or syllable, as: o'er, e'en, 't is, 't was, 't were, is't, know'st, and a few others such as 'mid, 'mongst, 'scape, 'gainst, 'ware. But these may also appear in triple measures in uncontracted form. This liberty is never extended to the printing of such words as "different" which Pope would contract to "diff'rent."

Browning did do some curious things, however, in eliding the consonants of the prepositions, "i' the" and "o' the," after the Elizabethan manner.[1] It was not a mannerism with him, but a serious attempt to indicate his own reading. Nevertheless he had no settled practice in the matter, and he would change the proof-sheets from "on" to "o'" and "o'" to "on" according to the emphasis he placed upon the words at the time.[2]

The only principle one can deduce from his practice (and there are two or three exceptions to it) is that if a measure contains four syllables the final consonant will be elided or slurred. This happens most frequently in the first measure after direct attack.

---

[1] "O' the" appears first in *Strafford*. "I' the" occurs once in *Paracelsus*. The consistent use of these forms develops in the later poems.

[2] *Living Age*, 244:407.

> Quivered i' the farthest rainbow-vapour, glanced
> (*Sord.* 2.25)
> —Jewels i' the locks that love no crownet like
> (*Sord.* 3.699)
> Even i' the telling! Adverse Powers above,
> (*Balau.* 738)
> Master o' the mint and keeper of the keys
> (*Red C.* 2.812)
> Loftier i' the last, not more emancipate;
> (*Pr. H. S.* 1016)
> Merry i' the household! Death takes up the tune!
> (*Herakles* 806)
> Rubbish o' the rock, some diamond, much-worms prize,
> (*R&B* 9.511)

But it is true of other measures as well:

> Aim at still higher honour,—gabble o' the goose!
> (*R&B* 5.445)
> Quenched lay their cauldron, cowered i' the dust the crew,
> (*R&B* 1.578)
> She unlatched door, let all the devils o' the dark
> (*R&B* 5.1505)

Beyond this, there are no fixed rules, and the apostrophes seem to be temperamental. We find in one line:

> O' the color of a crime, inform us first!   (*R&B* 1.182)

and in another:

> Of the elephant who, brute beast though he were,
> (*R&B* 1.231)

In one:

> In the urn, or white or black, does drop a black,
> (*R&B* 1.1223)

and in another:

> I' the air, and catch again, and twirl about (*R&B* 1.33)

In one:

> And carried by the Prince o' the Power of the Air
> (*R&B* 1.561)

and in another:

> The worship of that prince o' the power o' the air
> (*Prince H. S.* 2120)

In one he will print:

> I' the face of the world, you found her; she could speak
>
> > (*R&B* 2.862)

and in another:

> Followed her parents i' the face o' the world.
>
> > (*R&B* 3.720)

where, if read as indicated, the line is reduced to four measures.

In fact there are several lines reduced to four measures by this process, if they be read as indicated. They appear to be mistakes; for normally the preposition would carry a light metrical stress to mark the time division. The apostrophe makes this impossible.

> One sees the pulpit o' the epistle side, (*Tomb St. P.* 21)
> But flirting flag-like i' the face o' the world
>
> > (*R&B* 3.888)
>
> Thinketh He dwelleth i' the cold o' the moon.
>
> > (*Caliban* 25)
>
> Flinging the breast-blade i' the face o' the Fisc,
>
> > (*R&B* 8.1565)
>
> Archbishop, who art under, i' the Church, (*R&B* 10.983)

In a few cases, where the metrical accent would naturally fall on the preposition, the printed elision causes confusion by forcing the accent back upon a normally unstressed syllable:

> O' the | quali | *ty o' the* | Court and | what it | likes
>
> > (*R&B* 8.1727)
>
> | Treatment and | discip | *line o' the* | harsher | sort?"
>
> > (*R&B* 4.1582)
>
> Was | ignorant | of the | immi | *nence o' the* | point
>
> > (*R&B* 9.757)

Without the elision, one would undoubtedly read:

> O' the | quality | of the | court and | what it | likes
> | Treatment and | discipline | of the | harsher | sort?

And there are also a few cases where, although the "o' the" would be most natural, it is omitted in favor of an ellipsis in the true Browningesque manner.   In the light of his usual practice, there is no real reason why he should avoid a natural triple by writing

I looking out of window on a tree   (*Inn* A. 3.79)

or

I' neck of him as I,—whom, soul and sense,

(*R&B* 11.709)

instead of

I looking out *o' the* window on a tree

or

I' *the* neck of him.

CHAPTER XI

ENJAMBMENT

ALTHOUGH many run-on lines occur in Browning,[1] they do not often represent sublime flights of poetic imagination soaring through many successive lines as they do, for instance, in Milton. Browning's blank verse is nearly all in the form of dramatic monologue, where, as we have seen, the texture of the verse is modified and its range strictly limited by the situation exploited and the character of the speaker. Enjambment becomes, for the most part, a choppy phrase or sentence divided between two lines after this manner:

"Because you've daubed enough
Bistre for backround.   (*Inn Album* 4.316-7)
            'T is all
Forgotten, all this ignobility,   (*Ibid* 320-21)
            "Goose
You truly are!   (*Ibid* 2.86-7)
            I warn
Back, in God's name!   (*Ibid* 7.89-90)
            Both of us
Blameworthy,—I first meet my punishment—
            (*Ibid* 7.69-70)
            I hope
That was a master-stroke!   (*Ibid* 7.179-80)
            Not for me
The chapman's chance!   (*Ibid* 7.45-6)
            Take it now
Its power to pain is past!   (*Ibid* 7.49-50)

These examples are all taken from *The Inn Album* which has the highest percentage of enjambment

---

[1] They range from *Caliban upon Setebos* and *Andrea del Sarto* with 18%, through *Sludge* and *Blougram* with 26%, *The Ring and the Book* with 30%, *Prince H. S.* with 36%, to *Pauline* with 46%, and *Paracelsus* with 48%.

(43%) of any of the long poems after Paracelsus.
Many of its sentences are exactly five measures long,
and would make good end-stopped lines if they were
placed differently on the pattern.

> Our troublesomest dreams die off ‖ In daylight: (4.572)
> I plump my purse ‖ With other people's pounds. (4.52)
> God has some end to serve ‖ Ere he suppress you! (4.671)
> 'T is God ‖ Must bear such secrets and disclose them.
> (5.215)
> I profess myself ‖ One fertile in resource.   (5.255)

Lines of this type swell the percentage tables some
metrists like to compile, but they do not show the
characteristic traditionally associated with enjambment in blank verse: i.e. the sense "variously drawn
out from one verse into another." They do, however,
obscure the formal division into metrical lines even if
they do not bind a series of lines into a verse-para-
graph. This is true also of the many lines in which
two words closely associated in thought and gram-
matical structure are divided between two lines, as:

> There's a thick
> Dusk undeveloped spirit (I've observed) (*Sludge* 30-31)
> When I was a mere child, my mother. . . that's
> Violante, . . .   (*R&B* 7.178-9)
> With bag and baggage thus did Dido once
> Decamp,—for more authority, a queen! (*R&B* 9.652-3)
> The author lacks
> Discretion, and his zeal exceeds: (*R&B* 9.1027-8)
> Poor Rome perversely lingered round, despite
> Instruction, for the sake of purblind love,—
> (*R&B* 10.1114-5)
> I find it easy to believe: and if
> At any fateful moment of the strange
> Adventure, . . .   (*R&B* 10.1166-8)
> "Friends,
> I absolutely and preemptorily
> Believe!"   (*Blougram* 243-5)

These examples could be continued endlessly. It is obvious that tables of percentages are in themselves quite inadequate for differentiating the metrical effect of poems. *Fra Lippo Lippi* has 24% of its lines enjambed, Blair's *The Grave* has 25%; but one is full of short nervous sentences over-lapping the metrical lines, and the other is in solemn paragraphs. *Ferishtah's Fancies* and *Samson Agonistes* each has 41% of its lines enjambed; but one soars and the other talks.

The whole story of enjambment in Browning's verse can be summed up by saying that the phrases and sentences often overlap the metrical line but they almost never rise from broken, colloquial speech to melodious passages of song. This rather obvious point may be interestingly and finally illustrated by setting side by side a passage from *The Inn Album* and one from *Paradise Lost* in which the number of run-on lines is the same (50%); but the Milton passage contains two sentences and the Browning one contains nine.

> *You* out of hand and sight and care of me
> These four years, whom I felt, knew, all the while. . .
> Oh, it's no superstition! It's a gift
> O' the gamester that he snuffs the unseen powers
> Which help or harm him. Well I knew what lurked,
> Lay perdue paralyzing me,—drugged, drowsed
> And damnified my soul and body both!
> Down and down, see where you have dragged me to,
> You and your malice! I was, four years since,
> —Well, a poor creature! I became a knave.
> I squandered my own pence: I plump my purse
> With other people's pounds. I practiced play
> Because I liked it: play turns labor now
> Because there's profit also in the sport.
> (Inn Album 4.42-55)

> This said unanimous, and other rites
> Observing none, but adoration pure,
> Which God likes best, into their inmost bower

Handed they went; and, eased the putting off
These troublesome disguises which we wear,
Straight side by side were laid; nor turned, I ween
Adam from his fair spouse, nor Eve the rites
Mysterious of connubial love refused:
Whatever hypocrites austerely talk
Of purity, and place, and innocence,
Defaming as impure what God declares
Pure, and commands to some, leaves free to all.
Our Maker bids increase; who bids abstain
But our destroyer, foe to God and Man?

(*Paradise Lost* 4.736-48)

PART THREE

CHAPTER XII

RHYMES

QUARRELS over Browning's rhymes, like so many other Browning quarrels, belong to a by-gone age. That age was profoundly disturbed over Browning's double and triple rhymes on such arresting sounds as *grunt is 't:contrapuntist;* or *ins and outs:thin sand doubts.* Oscar Wilde, speaking for many intelligent readers of the day, could say in 1890, ". . . .rhyme, the one chord we have added to the Greek lyre, became in Robert Browning's hands a grotesque, misshapen thing, which made him at times masquerade in poetry as a low comedian, and ride Pegasus too often with his tongue in his cheek." [1]

But this statement is true only in the most limited way. It entirely forgets that Browning could also strike the new chord with as much genius and artistry as any other English poet, and that the memorable poems like *Evelyn Hope, "How They Brought the Good News," Prospice, Rabbi Ben Ezra,* and *Love Among the Ruins,* are perfect in the beauty and harmony of their rhymes. But there is nothing of importance to be said about these, because they are in common usage and do not distract the attention. Unfortunately the good and perfect things have been dwarfed by the ingenious, jocose, and sometimes absurd rhymes which irritated Wilde. It is these objectionable rhymes which call attention to themselves that have caused all the discussion; but, like the fly in the ointment, they are more striking than numerous.

[1] Richardson, *A Study of English Rhyme,* p. 185 (Quoted from the *Nineteenth Century* for July, 1890.)

The questions they raise in a study of Browning's versification are not recondite and perhaps not even very important.

If one wishes to be quite scientific after the German manner, he may dispose of the question in this way: There are 34,746 rhymes in Browning's poetry.[2] This represents two-fifths of his total output. Of this grand total there are but 322 which might be called either imperfect rhymes *(angered:vanguard; office:trophies)*, or forced rhymes *(equals: weak walls; shall see:palsy; from mice:promise; rims on:crimson)*. That is, less than one in a hundred is unusual, and the judgments against Browning's use of rhyme are based on this small percentage.

These 322 rhymes are, moreover, confined to a dozen and a half poems which are frankly humorous, or in which the character assumed to speak or the situation exploited naturally permit license in rhyme. Rhymes like, *Giotto:was it not O, wish you:issue,* in *Old Pictures in Florence; Holy Scriptures:see equipt yours, Manchester:haunches stir,* in *Christmas Eve; good humor:to do more, that's all:begat Saul, news of her: Lucifer,* in *The Flight of the Duchess; Italy:Spit ally, Gressoney:lesson eh,* in *Prologue to Ferishtah's Fancies;* or anything you wish from that wilderness of *Pacchiarotto*—such rhymes are indispensable to the effect of poems of this type, and they do not "profane the mysteries" or break the illusion. When, in *The Flight of the Duchess,* the mood changes or the characters shift, the rhymes change also. But the perfection of the speech of the Gipsy (lines 567 ff.) with its melodious rhymes is forgotten in the vagaries of the old hunter with his *"jerkin: work in"* rhymes.

[2] E. M. Clark, *Poet Lore* 2:480 ff. has done the counting and we take her word for it. Her excellent paper says nearly all there is to be said on this subject and we have leaned heavily upon it.

Such an analysis at least puts forward the facts, and the conclusions are not abstruse. One side of Browning shows a boyish humorist who loved to amuse his friends by finding rhymes for supposedly rhymeless words. He was inordinately proud of his ability, and according to all report, loved to display it on every occasion; as when, on being challenged to rhyme both parties to Lord Roseberry's marriage he proudly offered

> Venus, sea-froth's child,
>> Playing old gooseberry
>> Married Lord Roseberry
> To Hannah de Rothschild.
>> *(Living Age,* 261;658)

This was the Browning who loved the quaint, the odd, the jocose; who loved to "hitch into verse" these humors, shocks, and surprises. But the surprises are almost without exception reserved for the moments of indulgence. In its own way, *Pachiorotto* is as perfect as *Love Among the Ruins.* He is making use of the principle Coleridge set down in the *Biographia Literaria,* that "double and trisyllable rhymes, indeed, form a lower species of wit, and, attended to exclusively for their own sake, may become a source of momentary amusement; as in poor Smart's distich to the Welsh Squire who had promised him a hare:

> "Tell me, thou son of great Cadwallader!
> Hast sent the hare? or hast thou swallow'd her?"

If one agrees that a poet may be permitted an indulgence of this sort (and one in a hundred is proportionately few), one must admit that these are touched with the magic of genius, and have become instead of a "source of momentary amusement," a creation of art which no lover of Browning would willingly lose.

CHAPTER XIII

STANZA FORMS

Two-Line Stanzas

THE TWO-LINE stanza is as rare in Browning as elsewhere in English poetry, *The Boy and the Angel* being the only poem in this form.

> Morning, evening, noon and night,
> "Praise God!" sang Theocrite.
> Then to his poor trade he turned,
> Whereby the daily meal was earned.
> Had he labored, long and well;
> O'er his work the boy's curls fell.

The difference between this form and the regular tetrameter couplets is, in Browning, structural as well as typographical.[1] For his couplets run on and on until half of them are enjambed, while in *The Boy and the Angel* all but ten of the lines are end-stopped, and each couplet is "closed." This sets it quite apart from the other couplets and justifies the short stanza form.

Three-Line Stanzas

The tercet, rhymed aaa, has never been long without admirers among the poets. Browning favored it, with varying movements and line lengths, in eight poems. Although each stanza is often complete in itself, the thought very frequently overflows into the next stanza, linking two into one except for the printing. This is, however, much more usual in the strict *terza rima* where the overflow is a recognized part of the technique.

[1] See Chapter XIV.

It occurs in duple-triple tetrameters in *Rephan:*

> Can your world's phrase, your sense of things
> Forth-figure the Star of my God? No springs,
> No winters throughout its space. Time brings
>
> No hope, no fear: as to-day, shall be
> Tomorrow; advance or retreat need we
> At our stand-still through eternity?   (37-43)

It is used again in the rapidly moving four-measure dipodic line of *A Toccata of Galuppi's:*

> Oh Galuppi, Baldassare, this is very sad to find!
> I can hardly misconceive you; it would prove me deaf
>   and blind;
> But although I take your meaning, 't is with such a
>   heavy mind!

It occurs once in iambic pentameter:

> Witless alike of will and way divine,
> How heaven's high with earth's low should intertwine!
> Friends, I have seen through your eyes: now use mine!
>   (*Epilogue to Dramatis Personae*, 3rd speaker)

The six-measure line in duple-triple movement oc-curs in *Echetlos*, and with variations in *Up at a Villa —Down in the City;* i.e. the first two stanzas are ter-cets, the third adds a fourth line on the same rhyme, the fourth combines two tercets, etc. The line is, almost without exception, divided sharply by the cesura into two trimeters.

> Here is a story shall stir you! Stand up, Greeks dead
>   and gone,
> Who breasted, beat Barbarians, stemmed Persia rolling
>   on,
> Did the deed and saved the world, for the day was
>   Marathon!   (*Echetlos*)

The seven-measure line occurs in *White Witchcraft* and in *The Pope and the Net.*[2] It fails to give the feel-

---

[2] The Epilogues to *The Melon-Seller* and *Shah Abbas* are in this form.

ing of a tercet, however, because it falls naturally into tetrameter and trimeter, or ballad measure:

> If you and I could change to beasts, what beasts should
>   either be?
> Shall you and I play Jove for once? Turn fox then,
>   I decree!
> Shy wild sweet stealer of the grapes! Now do your
>   worst on me!   (*White Witchcraft*)

In like manner, the eight-measure trochaic lines of the epilogue to *The Family* fall into tetrameter with intermittent rhyme:

> Man I am and man would be, Love—merest man and
>   nothing more.
> Bid me seem no other! Eagles boast of pinions—let
>   them soar!
> I may put forth angel's plumage, once unmanned, but
>   not before.

Terza rima had been favored by Shelley, with slight modifications, in the *Ode to the West Wind, Prince Athanase, The Triumph of Life, The Woodman and the Nightingale,* etc. It is represented in Browning by *Doctor—* and *Jochanan Hakkadosh;* and in duple-triple tetrameters in *The Statue and the Bust.* Each stanza is linked to the preceding one by the rhyme scheme aba bcb cdc, etc. The division into stanzas is arbitrary, since the sense flows on continuously. In *Doctor—,* fifty-five of the eighty-five stanzas run on.

> "What is the fault now?" "This I find to blame:
> Many and various are the tongues below,
> Yet all agree in one speech, all proclaim
> " 'Hell has no might to match what earth can show:
> Death is the strongest-born of Hell, and yet
> Stronger than Death is a Bad Wife, we know.'
>   (*Doctor—4-9*)

The duple-triple tetrameter speeds up the verse of *The Statue and the Bust,* giving it a lighter touch than

the true pentameter terza rima.   The stanzas do not
run on into each other in this poem as they do in the
others.

> There's a palace in Florence, the world knows well,
> And a statue watches it from the square,
> And this story of both the townsmen tell.
>
> Ages ago, a lady there,
> At the farthest window facing the East
> Asked, "Who rides by with the royal air?"

The Four-Line Stanza

The quatrain has always been one of the staple verse
forms of English poetry.   It is capable of many variations in rhyme scheme, line length, and verse movement, and is therefore adapted to the individuality of
widely different poets.   It is, as one would expect, one
of Browning's most favored stanza forms; but it does
not preponderate over all other forms as it does in
many poets—Wordsworth for example.

On the couplet rhyme aabb it occurs in anapestic
tetrameter in *The Laboratory:*[3]

> Now, take all my jewels, gorge gold to your fill,
> You may kiss me, old man, on my mouth if you will!
> But brush this dust off me, lest horror it brings
> Ere I know it—next moment I dance at the King's!

The six-measure lines have a strong tendency to
break in the middle; it is difficult, therefore, to preserve the feeling of a quatrain in them.   This is especially noteworthy in the trochaic movement of *Before,* and the epilogue to *The Eagle,* where the cesura
after the sixth syllable pulls many of the lines into
seven measures, with the fourth monosyllabic:

> Let them fight it out, friend! things have gone too far.
> God must judge the couple: leave them as they are
> —Whichever one's the guiltless, to his glory,
> And whichever one the guilt's with, to my story! (*Before*)

[3] It is characteristic of Browning that the first verse should not set the
norm for the movement of the poem.

In the duple-triple movement of *Solomon and Balkis,* and *Halbert and Hob,* the break in the line is only a little less conspicuous. The stanza form is the same.

> Solomon King of the Jews and the Queen of Sheba, Balkis,
> Talk on the ivory throne, and we well may conjecture their talk is
> Solely of things sublime: why else has she sought Mount Zion,
> Climbed the six golden steps, and sat betwixt lion and lion?

The seven-measure lines with couplet rhymes fall easily into "common" measure:

> My grandfather says he remembers he saw, ‖ when a youngster long ago,
> On a bright May day, a strange old man, ‖ with a beard as white as snow,
> Stand on the hill outside our town ‖ like a monument of woe,
> And striking his bare bald head the while, ‖ sob out the reason—so!
>
> *(Martin Relph)*

The quatrain occurs more often in alternate rhyme than in any other form. It is the stanzaic basis of twenty-five of his poems. It appears in iambic movement with trimeter lines alternating with tetrameter ($a_4b_3a_4b_3$), as in *The Lost Mistress:* [4]

> All's over, then: doth truth sound bitter
>   As one at first believes?
> Hark, 't is the sparrows' good-night twitter
>   About your cottage eaves!

and in anapestic movement with double rhymes in *Muckle-Mouth Meg:*

---

[4] "You'll love me yet!—and I can tarry" (*Pippa Passes* III) is in this form. *Confessions,* and *Pambo* are the same except for a few triples and the double rhymes of *Pambo.*

> Frowned the Laird on the Lord: "So, red-handed I
>   catch thee?
> Death-doomed by our Law of the Border!
> We've a gallows outside and a chiel to dispatch thee:
>   Who trespasses—hangs: all's in order."

Frequently all four lines are tetrameter. This form occurs in iambic movement in *Bad Dreams I.*

> Last night I saw you in my sleep:
>   And how your charm of face was changed!
> I asked, "Some love, some faith you keep?"
>   You answered, "Faith gone, love estranged."

In all the other examples *(Prologue to Pacchiarotto, House, Dubiety, Epilogue to Mihrab Shah)*, the movement is duple-triple.

> Shall I sonnet-sing you about myself?
>   Do I live in a house you would like to see?
> Is it scant of gear, has it store of pelf?
>   "Unlock my heart with a sonnet-key?"   *(House)*

The trimeter lines are equally popular with the tetrameter. They are either in the short and choppy iambic movement of *The Twins, Ben Karshook's Wisdom,* and the *Prologue to Fifine at the Fair;* or the duple-triple movement of *Youth and Art,* and the epilogue to *A Camel-Driver.*

> Grand rough old Martin Luther
>   Bloomed fables—flowers on furze,
> The better the uncouther:
>   Do roses stick like burrs?   *(The Twins)*

> It once might have been, once only:
>   We lodged in a street together,
> You, a sparrow on the housetop lonely,
>   I, a lone she-bird of his feather.
>   *(Youth and Art)*

In two happy experiments—*Prologue to The Two Poets of Croisic,* and *A Woman's Last Word*—Brown-

ing combined trimeter and dimeter into a quatrain
with alternate rhyme.[5]

> World—how it walled about
>> Life with disgrace
> Till God's own smile came out:
>> That was thy face!   *(Prologue)*

> Be a god and hold me
>> With a charm!
> Be a man and fold me
>> With thine arm!   *(Woman's Last Word)*

The stanzas of *Memorabilia* and *A Light Woman* are
made up of three tetrameter lines and a trimeter, the
former in iambic, the latter in duple-triple movement.

> Ah, did you once see Shelley plain,
>> And did he stop and speak to you,
> And did you speak to him again?
>> How strange it seems and new!   *(Memorabilia)*

> So far as our story approaches the end,
>> Which do you pity the most of us three?—
> My friend, or the mistress of my friend
>> With her wanton eyes, or me?   *(A Light Woman)*

The pentameter quatrain is used but once in the
trochaic movement of *Fears and Scruples*.[6]

> Here's my case. Of old I used to love him,
>> This same unseen friend, before I knew:
> Dream there was none like him, none above him,—
>> Wake to hope and trust my dream was true.

The *Epilogue to Ferishtah's Fancies, Poetics,* and
Magical Nature, experiment with a combination of

[5] Some of the trimeters, because of the movement and the cesura, tend to
lengthen into tetrameter:

> Let's contend no more, Love,
>> Strive nor weep:
> All be as before, Love,
>> —Only sleep!

[6] *Pictor Ignotus,* the second speaker in the Epilogue to *Dramatis Personae,*
and *Bifurcation,* are printed as continuous verse.

six- and seven-measure lines in trochaic movement ($a_6b_7a_6b_7$) which suggests Poulter's measure:

> Then the cloud-rift broadens, spanning earth that's under,
>   Wide our world displays its worth, man's strife and
>   strife's success;
> All the good and beauty, wonder crowning wonder,
>   Till my heart and soul applaud perfection, nothing less.
> *(Epilogue)*

The quatrain with enclosed rhyme occurs once, in *Parting at Morning:* [7]

> Round the cape of a sudden came the sea,
> And the sun looked over the mountain's rim:
> And straight was a path of gold for him,
> And the need of a world of men for me.

A Pretty Woman, with its dimeters and its double and triple rhymes, does not give the effect of a quatrain.[8]

> That fawn-skin-dappled hair of hers,
>   And the blue eye
>   Dear and dewy,
> And that infantine fresh air of hers!
>   . . .   .
> So, we leave the sweet face fondly there:
>   Be its beauty
>   Its sole duty!
> Let all hope of grace beyond, lie there!
>   (Stanzas 1 and 7)

The quatrain with intermittent rhyme (xaya) occurs with irregular line length in prevailingly anapestic movement in *Donald*:

[7] The first two stanzas of *Helen's Tower* have this form, but the last is arranged abc abc_5.

[8] Thomson thinks he finds the basis of this metre in the lesser ionic. There are difficulties, however, not the least being that it violates the integrity of the short lines. The metrical problems raised by the combinations of short lines in many of Browning's poems are not startling. He liked the effect of short refrain lines and used them. They are, almost without exception, complete end stopped lines. *The Rhythm of Speech*, 345-6.

Yet he was not dead when they picked next day
  From the gully's depth the wreck of him;
His fall had been stayed by the stag beneath
  Who cushioned and saved the neck of him.
                              (Stanza 49)

and in iambic tetrameter in *May and Death:*

I wish that when you died last May,
  Charles, there had died along with you
Three parts of spring's delightful things;
  Ay, and, for me, the fourth part too.

Quintains.

The quintain stanza has never been widely used by
the poets.   In the nineteenth century Wordsworth
had used it for *The Blind Highland Boy,* with the
rhyme aabba; and for *The Idiot Boy* and *Peter Bell,*
with the unconnected rhyme abccb.[9]   In this form the
first line never seems to be an integral part of the
stanza.

Thought Peter, what can mean all this?
Some ugly witchcraft must be here!
—Once more the Ass, with motion dull,
Upon the pivot of his skull
Turned round his long left ear. (*Peter Bell* 416-20)

Byron satirically adopted the *Peter Bell* scheme, but
Shelley tied the stanza together in his *Peter Bell the
Third* with the rhyme abaab (with exceptions).

Browning is the only English poet who has given
preference to the quintain stanza.   Twenty-nine poems,
in all moods and movements, from *Two in the Com-
pagna* to *Fust and His Friends,* have this stanza form.
With a single exception,[10] the fifth line always continues one of the quatrain rhymes, making a pleasing
and closely concatenated stanza.   This form must have

[9] This form is used but once by Browning, in the translation *The Blind
Man to the Maiden.* ($a_4b_3c_4c_4b_3$)
[10] *Dis Aliter Visum,* abcca.

appealed to Browning because of its enlarged scope
and its infinite capacity for variation.

It occurs in iambic movement with four tetrameters
and a trimeter on the rhymes ababa, in *Two in the
Campagna* and in *Popularity.*

> I wonder do you feel today
>> As I have felt since, hand in hand,
> We sat down on the grass, to stray
>> In spirit better through the land,
> This morn of Rome and May?
>>>> *(Two in the Compagna)*

More frequently the movement is duple-triple, either
with the fifth line trimeter, as in *By The Fireside* and
Gold Hair; or with all five trimeter, as in *The Patriot*
and *James Lee's Wife IX.*

> Too white, for the flower of life is red:
>> Her flesh was the soft seraphic screen
> Of a soul that is meant (her parents said)
>> To just see earth, and hardly be seen,
> And blossom in heaven instead.
>>>> *(Gold Hair)*

> There is nothing to remember in me,
>> Nothing I ever said with a grace,
> Nothing I did that you care to see,
>> Nothing I was that deserves a place
> In your mind, now I leave you, set you free.
>>>> *(James Lee's Wife IX)*

It occurs once in trochaic movement, in *A Serenade
at the Villa.*

> That was I, you heard last night,
>> When there rose no moon at all,
> Nor, to pierce the strained and tight
>> Tent of heaven, a planet small:
> Life was dead and so was light.

The same rhyme scheme, ababa, occurs with duple-
triple trimeter in *Reverie:*

> I know there shall dawn a day
> —Is it here on homely earth?
> Is it yonder, worlds away,
> Where the strange and new have birth,
> That Power comes full in play?

in dactylic movement with combined trimeter and tetrameter, in *Master Hugues of Saxe-Gotha:*

> Hist, but a word, fair and soft!
> Forth and be judged, Master Hugues!
> Answer the question I've put you so oft:
> What do you mean by your mountainous fugues?
> See, we're alone in the loft,—

and in the still more elaborate combination of pentameters with tetrameter and trimeter, in *James Lee's Wife VI:*

> "Still ailing, Wind? Wilt be appeased or no?
> Which needs the other's office, thou or I?
> Dost want to be disburdened of a woe,
> And can, in truth, my voice untie
> Its links, and let it go?

In *The Worst of It* there is an interesting variation from this form. Browning has inserted an extra line with an internal rhyme different from the rhyme of the stanza.

> Would it were I had been false, not you!
> I that am nothing, not you that are all:
> I, never the worse for a touch or two
> On my speckled *hide;* not you, the *pride*
> Of the day, my swan, that a first fleck's fall
> On her wonder of white must unswan, undo!

The form ababb is equally in favor with Browning. It occurs in iambic tetrameter in *Shop, Bad Dreams IV,* and *Speculative.*

> That strong stern man my lover came
> —Was he my lover? Call him, pray,
> My life's cold critic bent on blame
> Of all poor I could do or say
> To make me worth his love one day—
>
> *(Bad Dreams IV)*

Porphyria's Lover and *Johannes Agricola in Meditation* are in this same form, but with the twelve stanzas of each printed together as continuous lines. In the *Prologue to Asolando* the fifth line is trimeter.

It occurs in anapestic movement in *Apollo and the Fates* and *Fust and his Friends:*

> Thy tongue slides to "comfort" already? Not mine!
> Behoove us deal roundly: the wretch is distraught
> —Too well I guess wherefore! Behooves a Divine
> —Such as I, by grace, boast me—to threaten one caught
> In the enemy's toils,—setting "comfort" at naught.
> *(Fust and His Friends)*

and in duple-triple trimeter in *Bad Dreams II* and the *Epilogue to Dramatis Personae* (First Speaker).

> You in the flesh and here—
> Your very self! Now, wait!
> One word! May I hope or fear?
> Must I speak in love or hate?
> Stay while I ruminate! *(Bad Dreams II)*

The form abaab occurs in duple-triple movement with a combination of tetrameter and trimeter lines, in *James Lee's Wife IV:*

> I will be quiet and talk with you,
> And reason why you are wrong.
> You wanted my love—is that much true?
> And so I did love, so I do:
> What has come of it all along?

and in trochaic tetrameter in the epilogue to *A Pillar at Sebzevar:* [11]

> Ask not one least word of praise!
> Words declare your eyes are bright?
> What then meant that summer day's
> Silence spent in one long gaze?
> Was my silencé wrong or right?

[11] The Epilogue to the second Series of *Dramatic Idyls,* and the album verses added to it: "Touch him ne'er so lightly, into song he broke:" are also rhymed ababb. The movement is trochaic hexameter.

Other forms are: iambic tetrameter rhymed aabba:

> "Bystanders reason, think of wives
> And children ere they risk their lives.
> Over the balustrade has bounced
> A mere instinctive dog, and pounced
> Plumb on the prize. 'How well he dives!
> *(Tray)*

abcca:

> Stop, let me have the truth of that!
> Is that all true? I say, the day
> Ten years ago when both of us
> Met on a morning, friends—as thus
> We meet this evening, friends or what?—
> *(Dis Aliter Visum)*

abbaa with combined trimeter and dimeter:

> All I believed is true!
> I am able yet
> All I want, to get
> By a method as strange as new:
> Dare I trust the same to you? *(Mesmerism)*

and aabab, with two short refrain lines, in *Rosny:*

> Woe, he went galloping into the war,
> Clara, Clara
> Let us two dream: shall he 'scape with a scar?
> Scarcely disfigurement, rather a grace
> Making for manhood which nowise we mar:
> See, while I kiss it, the flush on his face—
> Rosny, Rosny!

The Six-Line Stanza

The poets have, as a rule, always preferred the six-line stanza to the quintain; but Browning uses it less often. Twenty-two of his poems are in this form. They may take any one of a dozen different arrangements, though the most favored forms are the tetrameter lines rhymed ababcc (as in *Song, Count Gismond, Appearances,* parts of *Nationality in Drinks,* and, except for the second line in trimeter, the *Epilogue to the Two Poets of Croisic*) ; and the tetrameter couplets[12] (as in *"How They Brought The Good News from Ghent to Aix," Confessional, Holy-Cross Day, Humility,* and *One Way of Love.*[13])

> Nay but you, who do not love her,
>   Is she not pure gold, my mistress?
> Holds earth aught—speak truth—above her?
>   Aught like this tress, see, and this tress,
> And this last fairest tress of all,
> So fair, see, ere I let it fall?   *(Song)*

> Fee, faw, fum! bubble and squeak!
> Blessedest Thursday's the fat of the week.
> Rumble and tumble, sleek and rough,
> Stinking and savory, smug and gruff,
> Take the church-road, for the bell's due chime
> Gives us the summons—'t is sermon-time!
>   *(Holy-Cross Day)*

A combination of tetrameter and trimeter occurs with couplet rhyme ($a_3a_3b_4b_4c_4c_3$) in *Adam, Lilith, and Eve;* and in the form $a_3b_3a_3b_4c_4c_4$ in *Which?*[14] *James Lee's Wife V* is a pleasing combination of dimeter with tetrameter and trimeter in the form $a_2b_2a_2b_4c_4c_3$.

The other forms are largely individual, as if shaped by the mood of the poet.[15] The form abcabc in iambic pentameter occurs in *James Lee's Wife VII.* The rhymes are too widely separated to be a very important element in the stanza structure.

> Oh, good gigantic smile o' the brown old earth,
>   This autumn morning! How he sets his bones
> To back i' the sun, and thrusts out knees and feet
> For the ripple to run over in its mirth;
>   Listening the while, where on the heap of stones
> The white breast of the sea-lark twitters sweet.

[12] In lines 104-115 of *In a Gondola* the arrangement is $aaaab_4b_3$.

[13] In this poem, the fifth line has an internal rhyme.

[14] Some of the stanzas begin with lines which read easily as trochaic tetrameter.

[15] Two stanzas of *In a Gondola* (37-48) have the arrangement $ababa_1a_2$.

This rhyme scheme (abcabc) is used with hexameter lines in *Muléykeh*, and the epilogue to *Two Camels;* and with five tetrameters and a trimeter ($abcab_4c_3$) in *Ponte Dell' Angelo, Venice.* It also occurs, with a happy combination of trimeter, tetrameter, and dimeter, in *St. Martin's Summer* ($a_3b_3c_4a_4b_4c_2$.).

> No protesting, dearest!
> Hardly kisses even!
> Don't we both know how it ends?
> How the greenest leaf turns seerest,
> Bluest outbreak—blankest heaven,
> Lovers—friends?

The rhyme rolls down and up like a wave on the scheme abccba in *Meeting at Night* [16]

> The gray sea and the long black land;
> And the yellow half-moon large and low;
> And the startled little waves that leap
> In fiery ringlets from their sleep,
> As I gain the cove with pushing prow,
> And quench its speed i' the slushy sand.

There is nothing very distinctive about the form $aabccb_5$ of *"Childe Roland to the Dark Tower Came."* *Rabbi Ben Ezra,* however, uses the *Any Wife to Any Husband* stanza with distinction by skillfully varying the line-lengths: $a_3a_3b_5c_3c_3b_6$.

> Grow old along with me!
> The best is yet to be,
> The last of life, for which the first was made;
> Our times are in his hand
> Who saith, "A whole I planned,
> Youth shows but half; trust God: see all, nor be afraid!"

The Seven-Line Stanzas

Browning's eight poems in seven-line stanzas are all in some way individual.[17] Even in the epilogue to

---

[16] Two stanzas of *In a Gondola* (1.203-214) are in this form.

[17] Two stanzas of *In a Gondola* (49-62) are arranged $a_2b_4b_3acca_4$.

The Bean Feast, where he uses the rhyme scheme and the iambic movement of the recognized rhyme royal (ababbcc$_5$), he varies the form by making the last line trimeter.

The only form used in a poem of sufficient length and body to give individuality to any one arrangement of the seven-line stanza is the iambic pentameter rhymed ababcca of *The Guardian Angel.*

> Dear and great Angel, wouldst thou only leave
>   That child, when thou hast done with him, for me!
> Let me sit all the day here, that when eve
>   Shall find performed thy special ministry,
> And time come for departure, thou, suspending,
> Thy flight, may'st see another child for tending,
>   Another still, to quiet and retrieve.

The arrangement ababccc$_4$, which is a combination of a quatrain and a tercet, is used in the two short poems, *Arcades Ambo,* and *The Lady and the Painter. Misconceptions* experiments in its two stanzas with a combination of trimeter and tetrameter with double rhymes (ababb$_3$a$_4$a$_4$). The two stanzes of *A Pearl, a Girl* are really sestains ababcc plus a refrain line x.[18]

The frail dimeters on the rhyme ababcbc in *James Lee's Wife I* are perfect in their way; and the combination of trimeter and dimeter with the intricate rhyme aabbaaa in *A Lovers' Quarrel* achieves some personality and distinction through the twenty-two stanzas:

> Ah, Love, but a day
>   And the world has changed!
> The sun's away,
>   And the bird estranged;
> The wind has dropped,
>   And the sky's deranged:
> Summer has stopped.   *(James Lee's Wife I)*

---

[18] The *Epitaph on Levi Lincoln Thaxter* has the form abaabba$_5$.

Oh, what a dawn of day!
How the March sun feels like May!
   All is blue again
   After last night's rain,
And the South dries the hawthorne-spray.
   , Only, my Love's away!
I'd as lief that the blue were gray.

(A Lovers' Quarrel)

The Eight-Line Stanzas

The eight line stanza is used in twenty-seven poems. It is usually nothing more than a double quatrain on the familiar rhymes. Thus, eight of the poems (*Garden Fancies, Evelyn Hope, Soliloquy of the Spanish Cloister, Old Pictures in Florence, The Heretic's Tragedy, At the "Mermaid," Filippo Baldinucci on the Privilege of Burial*, and the *Epilogue to Fifine at the Fair*)[19] are in double tetrameter quatrains abab cdcd; *The Incident of the French Camp* is composed of two quatrains in common measure ($a_4b_3a_4b_3$ etc.) ; *Fame* has two pentameter quatrains with alternate rhyme, and *Abt Vogler* has two hexameter quatrains. The same form is tried with success in double rhymed dimeter in *Pisgah-Sights:*

Over the ball of it,
   Peering and prying
How I see all of it,
   Life there, outlying!
Roughness and smoothness,
   Shine and defilement,
Grace and uncouthness:
   One reconcilement.

The two quatrains have intermittent rhyme (xaya etc.) in *Cristina,* and enclosed rhyme (abbacddc) in *Respectability.*[20] One of those happy uses of the dim-

---

[19] The *Founder of the Feast* has one eight- and one seven-line stanza abbaabba₅, abcabca₅.

[20] Two stanzas have an internal rhyme on d in the sixth line.

eter line occurs with this rhyme scheme in the prologue to *La Saisiaz:*

> Good, to forgive;
>   Best, to forget!
>   Living, we fret;
> Dying, we live.
> Fretless and free,
>   Soul, clap thy pinion!
>   Earth have dominion,
> Body, o'er thee!

The *ottava rima* stanza (iambic pentameter ababa-
bcc) is used with no special distinction in *The Two
Poets of Croisic,* and in *Pan and Luna.*

The other poems in the eight-line stanza are in some
way unusual.[21]   The complex structure: $a_3b_2c_4a_2d_3b_2$-c_4d_2, with the rhyme jumping over two or three lines
each time, has a beautiful effect in *In a Year:*

> Never any more,
>   While I live,
> Need I hope to see his face
>   As before.
> Once his love grown chill,
>   Mine may strive:
> Bitterly we re-embrace,
>   Single still.

Three dimeters and five tetrameters are combined on
the rhyme abcddabc to form the stanza of *Love in a
Life:*

> Room after room,
> I hunt the house through
> We inhabit together.
> Heart, fear nothing, for, heart, thou shalt find her—
> Next time, herself!—not the trouble behind her
> Left in the curtain, the couch's perfume!
> As she brushed it, the cornice-wreath blossomed anew:
> Yon looking-glass gleamed at the wave of her feather.

---

[21] *Deaf and Dumb* (aaabccb$_5$); *Eurydice to Orpheus* (aabccbdd$_5$); and
Summum Bonum (abab$_5$bc$_3$a$_5$c$_2$) have but a single stanza each.   The Epi-
logue to *Plot Culture* has two stanzas: ababccd$_5$d$_2$. *Through the Metidja to
Abd-el-Kadr,* in eight-line stanzas, is treated in Chapter XIX.

The form is varied in *James Lee's Wife II*, to $a_4b_2a_4c_2$-$c_2d_4d_4b_2$; the delayed b rhyme tying the stanza together.

The combination of trimeter and tetrameter, $a_3bcccba_4a_3$, forms the stanza of the *Epilogue to Pacchiarotto*. The six-, seven- and eight-measure lines ($a_6b_8a_6c_7d_6b_8d_6c_7$) of *Pietro of Abano* are constantly breaking up into two shorter lengths, so that the stanza has little unity. But the tetrameters of *Cristina and Monaldeschi*, with the closely linked rhyme abbbaccc, have some individuality:

> Since they witness to incessant
> Love like ours: King Francis, he—
> Diane the adored one, she—
> Prototypes of you and me.
> Everywhere is carved her Crescent
> With his Salamander-sign—
> Flame-fed creature: flame benign
> To itself or, if malign,

The descending and ascending rhymes abcddcab in the classical movement of duple-triple hexameters are used in *Pheidippides*. It makes a stately and dignified stanza.

> First I salute this soil of the blessed, river and rock!
> Gods of my birthplace, dæmons and heroes, honor to all!
> Then I name thee, claim thee for our patron, co-equal in
>   praise
> —Ay, with Zeus the Defender, with Her of the ægis and
>   spear!
> Also, ye of the bow and the buskin, praised be your peer,
> Now, henceforth and forever,—O latest to whom I upraise
> Hand and heart and voice! For Athens, leave pasture and
>   flock!
> Present to help, potent to save, Pan—patron I call!

Nine-Line Stanzas

The Spenserian is the only nine-line stanza which has had a recognized place in English poetry; the other forms have been shaped to meet the requirements of the individual poet without, however, establishing any one arrangement as an accepted type.[22]   Browning did not use the Spenserian stanza, nor did he invent any striking form of nine-line stanza in his three attempts at its use. *Apparent Failure* consists of two quatrains with an extra line on the d rhyme: $ababcdcdd_4$. *Natural Magic* is a little more complex with its two opening lines of trimeter, but it is really two quatrains with enclosed rhyme with the extra line at the beginning rhyming with the sixth and ninth: $ab_3ccbadda_4$.

Oh Love! Love is more intricate with its combinations of pentameter and trimeter with a closing alexandrine: $aabcb_5c_3d_5d_3c_6$.

> Oh Love! Love, thou that from the eyes diffusest
> Yearning, and on the soul sweet grace inducest—
> Souls against whom thy hostile march is made—
> Never to me be manifest in ire,
> Nor, out of time and tune, my peace invade!
> Since neither from the fire—
> No, nor from the stars—is launched a bolt more mighty
> Than that of Aphrodite
> Hurled from the hands of Love, the boy with Zeus for sire.

Stanzas of more than nine lines have no one established form.   Browning used a ten-line stanza in *Mary Wollstonecraft and Fuseli*.[23]   It is composed of a quatrain on alternate rhyme and three couplets: $ababccdde_4e_3$.

An eleven-line stanza appears in two poems.   In *The Last Ride Together* it is made up of four tetrameter couplets and a tercet, the third couplet being split to tie the stanza together: aabbcddeec.   In *Another Way of Love* it is composed of eight dimeters

---

[22] Tennyson's *Lady of Shalott;* Swinburne's *Tale of Balen, and Olive;* Rossetti's *The Portrait,* are nineteenth century examples.

[23] Gray's *Ode on a Distant Prospect of Eton College,* and Keat's *Ode to a Nightingale,* were excellent precedents.

rhymed abcddabc and a tercet eee. There is no structural unity to the stanza.

> June was not over
>   Though past the full,
> And the best of her roses
>   Had yet to blow,
> When a man I know
>   (But shall not discover,
> Since ears are dull,
>   And time discloses)
> Turned him and said with a man's true air,
> Half sighing a smile in a yawn, as 't were,—
> "If I tire of your June, will she greatly care?"[24]

The twelve-line stanzas of *Bad Dreams III* are composed of three tetrameter quatrains, the first and third on alternate rhymes, the second in couplets: ababccddefef. *Flute Music* is made up of three quatrains on alternate rhymes, with a nice combination of trimeter and tetrameter lines: $a_3b_3a_4b_3c_3d_3c_4d_3e_3f_3e_4f_3$.

> Ah, the bird-like fluting
>   Through the ash-tops yonder—
> Bullfinch-bubblings, soft sounds suiting
>   What sweet thoughts, I wonder?
> Fine-pearled notes that surely
>   Gather, dewdrop-fashion,
> Deep-down in some heart which purely
>   Secretes globuled passion—
> Passion insuppressive—
>   Such is piped, for certain;
> Love, no doubt, nay, love excessive
>   'Tis, your ash-tops curtain.

In *Too Late,* the other poem in this stanza form, the rhyme scheme of the last two quatrains is made a little more intricate by splitting the second: ababcdefefcd.

> Here was I with my arm and heart
>   And brain, all yours for a word, a want
> Put into a look—just a look, your part,—
>   While mine, to repay it. . . vainest vaunt,

[24] The rhymes in this first stanza are often imperfect.

Were the woman, that's dead, alive to hear,
    Had her lover, that's lost, love's proof to show!
But I cannot show it; you cannot speak
    From the churchyard neither, miles removed,
Though I feel by a pulse within my cheek,
    Which stabs and stops, that the woman I loved
Needs help in her grave and finds none near,
    Wants warmth from the heart which sends it—so!

The Sonnets

Browning wrote nine sonnets.[25] Three of these appear in humorous sequence as an epilogue to *Jochanan Hakkadosh;* the other six he himself did not reprint, and his literary judgment was unimpeachable. But pious though misguided enthusiasts must have all the saint's relics; Browningana is therefore enriched by these fugitive pieces. Browning's genius was not at home in the rigid limits of such a fixed form as the sonnet. Since he did not consider them worth reprinting, we may dismiss them with a word or two.

The first of these pieces, *Eyes, calm beside thee (Lady, couldst thou know!),* is eccentric in form. The rhymes are not perfect, but they follow the scheme abab ccab efa efa. In all the others the octave is alike: two quatrains with enclosed rhyme abba abba. The sestet is varied in four ways:

1—abba abba cde cde: *Helen's Tower, Jochanan III,*
                        Founder of the Feast[25]

2—   cde ced: *Rawdon Brown.*

3—   cdc dcd: *Jochanan I, II, Goldoni, Why I am*
                        a Liberal.

4—   cdc ddc: *The Names.*

[25] See Karl Lentzner's *Robert Browning's Sonettdichtung* Anglia XI, 500-17. Lentzner omits *Eyes Calm Beside Thee* but includes *The Founder of the Feast.* In the collected editions of Browning this poem has fifteen lines; Lentzner prints it as a sonnet by omitting one line:
    "Bach like Beethoven. Are we thankless, pray,
    To him whose every guest not idly vaunts, etc."

The most interesting thing about these pieces is that they illustrate in brief form the evolution of Browning's style. One needs only to set two of them side by side and they write the chapter. These two are just a half-century apart:

1834 (Aetat. 22)

Eyes, calm beside thee (Lady, couldst thou know!)
    May turn away thick with fast gathering tears:
I glance not where all gaze: thrilling and low
        Their passionate praises reach thee—my cheek wears
        Alone no wonder when thou passest by;
    Thy tremulous lids, bent and suffused, reply
To the irrepressible homage which doth glow
    On every lip but mine: if in thine ears
Their accents linger—and thou dost recall
    Me as I stood, still, guarded, very pale,
        Beside each votarist whose lighted brow
Wore worship like an aureole, "O'er them all
    My beauty," thou wilt murmur, "did prevail
        Save that one only"; Lady, couldst thou know!

1884 (Aetat. 72)

Sighed Rawdon Brown: "Yes, I'm departing, Toni!
    I needs must, just this once before I die,
    Revisit England: *Anglus* Brown am I,
Although my heart's Venetian. Yes, old crony—
Venice and London—London's 'Death the Bony'
        Compared with Life—that's Venice! What a sky,
        A sea, this morning! One last look! Good-by,
Cà Pesaro! No, lion—I'm a coney
To weep! I'm dazzled; 't is that sun I view
        Rippling the—the—*Cospetto*, Toni! Down
            With carpet-bag, and off with valise-straps!
'*Bella Venezia, non ti lascio più!*' "
        Nor did Brown ever leave her: well, perhaps
            Browning, next week, may find himself quite Brown!

Other Verse Forms

Besides these stanzas of definite line length, there are other poems, whose forms are entirely unique and individual, which must be mentioned separately. The *Cavalier Tunes* have such distinction.

I. *Marching Along* has six lines rhymed in couplets, with an added internal rhyme in the first, third, and fifth lines. The last two lines become the chorus for the other stanzas which have really only four lines.

> Kentish Sir Byng stood for his King,
> Bidding the crop-headed Parliament swing:
> And, pressing a troop unable to stoop
> And see the rogues flourish and honest folk droop,
> Marched them along, fifty-score strong,
> Great-hearted gentlemen, singing this song.

Strangely enough, in one section of *In a Gondola* (ll.63-78), "He" sings to this same tune. There is a slight variation in the form of the "chorus"; [26] the internal rhyme is lacking in one line and one measure is missing in the other. Otherwise the form is the same:

> What are we two?
> I am a Jew,
> And carry thee, farther than friends can pursue,
> To a feast of our tribe;
> Where they need thee to bribe
> The devil that blasts them unless he imbibe
> Thy. . . Scatter the vision forever! And now,
> As of old, I am I, thou art thou!

II. *Give a Rouse* is in quatrains with alternate double rhymes, and with the inspired chorus:

> King Charles, and who'll do him right now?
> King Charles, and who's ripe for fight now?
> Give a rouse: here's in hell's despite now,
> King Charles!

III. *Boot and Saddle* is really in tercets, the first line of the first stanza being repeated as a chorus:

---

26 The last two lines are repeated at the end of the second stanza.

> Boot, saddle, to horse, and away!
> Rescue my castle before the hot day
> Brightens to blue from its silvery gray.
>   Cho.—Boot, saddle, to horse, and away!

All four of the stanzas are rhymed on the same sound.

The Lost Leader is composed of two stanzas which combine four quatrains to make a sixteen-line stanza. The first quatrain has alternate rhyme abab; the last three have intermittent rhyme xaya.

"De Gustibus—" has two sections of uneven length. The first is printed in thirteen lines (the dimeters are split tetrameters with internal rhyme) thus:

$$a_4b_2b_2c_4c_4a_4d_2d_2e_4e_4e_2e_2e_2.$$

The second part is made up of tetrameter lines combining couplets, alternate and enclosed rhymes.

Home-Thoughts, From Abroad has an eight- and a twelve-line stanza, composed in the complex and individual form:

$$a_3b_3a_3c_4c_4c_4d_4d_3 \text{ and } a_4a_4b_5c_5b_5c_5d_5d_3e_:e_5f_5f_5$$

Life in a Love is distinctive because of its rhymes. The first three monopodies rhyme with the last three, though separated by sixteen tetrameter lines:

> Escape me?
> Never—
> Beloved!
> (Four unseparated quatrains abba cddc efef ghgh)
> I shape me—
> Ever
> Removed!

In Three Days is also highly individual. It is composed of four stanzas of uneven length (7, 7, 9, 15, lines). The first two lines:

> So I shall see her in three days
> And just one night, but nights are short,

are echoed down through the poem in the second and fourth stanzas with slight variation; and the first three lines become the closing ones, adding

> Then just two hours, and that is morn.

Women and Roses alternates a tercet (aaa$_3$) with an eight-line stanza rhymed in couplets (aabbccdd$_4$), plus a refrain line x.

I

> I dream of a red-rose tree.
> And which of its roses three
> Is the dearest rose to me?

II

> Round and round, like a dance of snow
> In a dazzling drift, as its guardians, go
> Floating the women faded for ages,
> Sculptured in stone, on the poet's pages.
> Then follow women fresh and gay,
> Living and loving and loved today,
> Last, in the rear, flee the multitude of maidens,
> Beauties yet unborn.   And all, to one cadence,
> They circle their rose on my rose tree.

This combination is repeated four times.

After and *Instans Tyrannus* alternate an anapestic trimeter with a dimeter on the same rhyme in stanzas of unequal length.

I

> Of the million or two, more or less,
> I rule and possess,
> One man, for some cause undefined,
> Was least to my mind.
>
> *(Instans Tyrannus)*

The lovely lyrics in that anthology entitled *In a Gondola* have been mentioned separately in their appropriate places.

Waring has no definite stanza structure; it skillfully combines trimeters and tetrameters in couplet and quatrain rhymes. The few pentameters and dimeters are somewhat accidental:

> Ay, most likely 't is in Spain
> That we and Waring meet again
> Now, while he turns down that cool narrow lane
> Into the blackness, out of grave Madrid
> All fire and shine, abrupt as when there's slid
> Its stiff gold blazing pall
> From some black coffin lid.
> Or best of all,
> I love to think
> The leaving us was just a feint; (*Waring* 135-144)

Hervé Riel is a "ballad" in stanzas of uneven length, no two of which are just alike. They have no unusual distinction.

Wanting Is—What? is composed of a six line stanza in dactylic tetrameter enclosed by two dimeter quatrains. A refrain echo "Grows love!" closes the poem.

> Wanting is—what?
> Summer redundant,
> Blueness abundant,
> —Where is the blot?
> Beamy the world, yet a blank all the same,
> —Framework which waits for a picture to frame:
> What of the leafage, what of the flower?
> Roses embowering with naught they embower!
> Come then, complete incompletion, O comer,
> Pant through the blueness, perfect the summer!
> Breathe but one breath
> Rose-beauty above,
> And all that was death
> Grows life, grows love,
> Grows love!

Browning had a great fondness for short echo lines following longer ones. *Love Among the Ruins* is the most musical as it is the most beautiful poem in this arrangement. It is divided into stanzas composed of six long and six short lines, each short one rhyming

with the preceding long one.   The length of the first
line, and the couplet rhyme, emphasize the echo effect
of the second.

> Where the quiet-colored end of evening smiles
>   Miles and miles
> On the solitary pastures where our sheep
>   Half-asleep
> Tinkle homeward through the twilight, stray or stop
>   As the crop—
> Was the site once of a city great and gay,
>   (So they say)
> Of our country's very capital, its prince
>   Ages since
> Held his court in, gathered councils, wielding far
>   Peace or war.

The Englishman in Italy is less ethereal in its music.
It is, as a matter of fact, the *Saul* line broken into a
trimeter and a dimeter; [27] but the conflict between the
metre and the phrases is more nearly mortal.

> But to-day not a boat reached Salerno,
>   So back, to a man,
> Came our friends, with whose help in the vineyards
>   Grape-harvest began.
>   (*ll.* 69-72)
>
> How good is man's life, the mere living!
>   how fit to employ
> All the heart and the soul and the senses
>   forever in joy!   (*Saul* 78-79)

Prospice combines tetrameter and dimeter lines on
alternate rhymes.   This combination, in duple-triple
movement, suggests the effect of classic hexameters: [28]

> Fear death?—to feel the fog in my throat,
>   The mist in my face,
> When the snows begin, and the blasts denote
>   I am nearing the place,

[27] *After,* and *Instans Tyrannus,* are in the same form except for rhyme.
The first two lines of each stanza of *James Lee's Wife III,* are in the same
form.

[28] See Chapter XVIII, p. 179.

> The power of the night, the press of the storm,
>> The post of the foe;
> Where he stands, the Arch Fear in a visible form,
>> Yet the strong man must go:
>>> (*Prospice* 1-8)

In the *Prologue to Ferishtah's Fancies,* and in *A Grammarian's Funeral,* the short line, instead of continuing the same movement and echoing the effect of the long one, introduces a new movement which is likely to disturb the even flow of the expected metre. These two poems show how completely different may be the effect of what is theoretically the same verse form.[29]

> Let us begin and carry up this corpse,
>> Singing together,
> Leave we the common crofts, the vulgar thorpes
>> Each in its tether
> Sleeping safe on the bosom of the plain,
>> Cared-for till cock-crow:
> Look out if yonder be not day again
>> Rimming the rock-row!
>>> (*Grammarian's Funeral*)

> Pray, Reader, have you eaten ortolans
>> Ever in Italy?
> Recall how cooks there cook them: for my plan's
>> To—Lyre with Spit ally.
> They pluck the birds,—some dozen luscious lumps,
>> Or more or fewer,—
> Then roast them, heads by heads and rumps by rumps,
>> Stuck on a skewer.
>>> (*Prologue to Ferishtah*)

The freedom and irregularity of *My Star* are more apparent than real. The first eight lines are duple-triple diameter with alternate rhymes (ababcdcd). The ninth line lengthens into a tetrameter, though it is bound to the dimeter quatrain by rhyme. The final

---

[29] The effect of the adonic has been discussed in Chapter III.

tetrameter quatrain (which is not merely two dimeters printed as one line) sweeps the poem to a rich,
melodious ending, as though the aspiration of the early
dimeters had attained metrical fulfillment.

> All that I know
>   Of a certain star
> Is, it can throw
>   (Like the angled spar)
> Now a dart of red,
>   Now a dart of blue;
> Till my friends have said
>   They would fain see, too,
> My star that dartles the red and the blue!
> Then it stops like a bird; like a flower, hangs furled:
>   They must solace themselves with the Saturn above it.
> What matter to me if their star is a world?
>   Mine has opened its soul to me; therefore I love it.

CHAPTER XIV

THE COUPLETS

The Pentameter Couplet

There are two types of pentameter couplets in English poetry: the open form of *Endymion,* and the closed form of *The Essay On Man.* The open form could be accurately described, if the paradox might be indulged, as blank verse with rhyme; for the stream of thought overflows the confines of the lines and runs on into the next and the next until, like good blank verse, it is felt in paragraphs rather than in lines or couplets. The closed couplet, on the other hand, is compressed, epigrammatic, snappy, antithetical, composed and felt in units of two lines coupled by rhyme. Even when the thought is developed through several lines, it is built up of separate couplet units like so many chiseled stones in an archway. The "All nature is but art unknown to thee" passage is a good and classic example.

Of these two types, Browning, as the reader might suppose, chose the open couplet. Approximately ten per cent of his work is in this form. *Sordello* is the only poem of great length; the *Parleyings* which, taken together, are not quite half as long as *Sordello,* are really seven separate poems of about four hundred lines each. The other nine poems in pentameter couplets are comparatively short, ranging from the eight lines of *Fame,* to the three hundred ninety-six of *A Forgiveness.* Only one of this group is in strict heroic couplets—the eight lines of *Fame:*

> See, as the prettiest graves will do in time,
> Our poet's wants the freshness of its prime;
> Spite of the sexton's browsing horse, the sods
> Have struggled through its binding osier rods;
> Headstone and half-sunk footstone lean awry,
> Wanting the brick-work promised by-and-by;
> How the minute gray lichens, plate o'er plate,
> Have softened down the crisp-cut name and date!

All the rest are more or less open.

Browning's pentameter couplets have two noteworthy characteristics: their openness and their comparative regularity. They are in no sense heroic couplets; they are distinguished from regular blank verse in nothing but rhyme, and the observations on blank verse apply as well to them. The couplets are wide open. The thought lengthens out from one line into another until sixty per cent of the lines are enjambed. The rhymes are not only unobtrusive, but they frequently leave the reader quite unaware of their presence. Unfamiliar readers are likely to read *My Last Duchess* with the impression of blank verse. A quotation at this point would invalidate the experiment; the reader should, if possible, get interested in a passage from *Sordello,* and after finishing it, ask himself whether or not he was aware of rhyme. But we may for convenience give here an illustration of the open structure of the couplet.

> The sire led in
> A son as cruel; and this Ecelin
> Had sons, in turn, and daughters sly and tall
> And curling and compliant; but for all
> Romano (so they styled him) throve, that neck
> Of his so pinched and white, that hungry cheek
> Proved 'twas some fiend, not him, the man's-
> 　　flesh went
> To feed: whereas Romano's instrument,

Famous Taurello Salinguerra, sole
I' the world, a tree whose boughs were slipt
    the bole
Successively, why should not he shed blood
To further a design?

(*Sordello* 1.275-286)

In this representative passage the cesuras are so skillfully shifted about, and the phrase units are so carefully distributed through the line and across the lines that only three (277, 282, 285) are in any sense complete on the rhyme word. The rhyme has become purely ornamental in contrast to the organic quality of the rhyme in the heroic couplet.

As if the rhymes were not already reticent enough, Browning often obscures them still further by hiding them away in alternate and enclosed schemes as variants from the continuous couplet form. Could rhymed pentameters be more nearly like blank verse and still be rhymed pentameters than, say, such a passage as this from *Christopher Smart?*

                  . . . with me first glance
Was but full recognition that in trance
Or merely thought's adventure some old day
Of dim and done-with boyishness, or—well,
Why might it not have been, the miracle
Broke on me as I took my sober way
Through veritable regions of our earth
And made discovery, many a wondrous one?

II

Anyhow, fact or fancy, such its birth:
I was exploring some huge house, had gone
Through room and room complacently, ...

The rhyme scheme would be aa bccb de de etc., and even this unobtrusive scheme is subordinated by such imperfect rhymes as *well:miracle; one:gone.*

The other singularity of the pentameter couplets is the extreme regularity of the versification, especially when compared with the irregularities of the blank verse. In these poems Browning relies almost wholly upon the traditional and the universally accepted variations from the normal iambic pattern as enumerated and illustrated in Chapter V. It would be repeating the obvious to multiply further illustration. Even *Sordello,* which is less regular than the rest, seldom has a triple except in the first measure after a direct attack or before or after a monosyllabic measure. In marked contrast to his freedom from rigid rules in his blank verse, he seems to have felt himself bound to them when he wrote the couplet. Except for the rare use of "o' the" and "i' the" [1] the triples are not insistent; and examples of two triples in one line are few and far between. Book One yields these:

> Plucker of amaranths grown beneath God's eye (1.371)
> Over the woods to Mantua: there he strolled. (1.621)
> Summers, and winters quietly came and went. (1.697)
> O' the instant, more with earlier loves to wrench (1.933)
> The vein-streaks swollen a richer violet where   (1.956)

and Book Two these:

> Brightened, "as in the slumbrous heart o' the woods (2.4)
> The sorriest bat which cowers throughout noontide (2.228)
> Strangle some day with a cross olive-stone!   (2.422)
> Sunning himself o' the slime where whirrs the breeze—"
>   (2.773)

Not one of these lines is very striking; and only one would be out of place in a Popean couplet. The others are usually direct attack, making the first measure triple, and easily elided syllables which distinctly tone down the triple effect.

A single triple measure is also comparatively rare, and usually of the type:

> Into a *sumptuous* swell of gold and wound   (1.949)
> All out except a floating *power,* a name   (4.972)

---

[1] These occur in 54 lines in *Sordello;* one line contains both.

In the *Parleyings* there are whole poems in which the only triple measures are such easy elisions as "heaven and," "the instructor," "flower and," etc. In the blank verse pentameters these were so common that they became a part of the basic pattern.

The Tetrameter Couplet

Browning made but little use of the tetrameter couplet; his genius preferred the wider freedom of the mightier pentameter to the close restriction of the tetrameter with its almost unavoidable sing-song metre and its obtrusive rhymes. The shorter poems in four-measure lines, such as *The Confessional,* and *One Way of Love,* are not strictly tetrameter couplets, inasmuch as they are cast into definite stanza forms.[2] *The Last Ride Together* falls outside of this group because the fifth line of each stanza rhymes with the eleventh, and the eighth, ninth, and tenth have the same rhyme. *In A Gondola* is only partly in tetrameter couplets. This leaves *Christmas Eve* and *Easter Day,* and *The Italian in England* as the true representatives of the form.[3]

And even *Christmas Eve* cannot be admitted without some important qualifications. It is not octosyllabic like *Easter Day;* and it is iambic only in certain passages of its 1359 lines. It is more like Coleridge's *Christabel,* for the accents remain constant in number while the syllables range from eight to thirteen. It is therefore more accurately described as duple-triple rhythm.[4] The rhymes are prevailingly double and often strikingly eccentric:

> Besides, you go gently all the way uphill.
> . . . .
> My head grew lighter, my limbs more supple, (209, 211)

[2] *One Way of Love* is further differentiated by the internal rhyme in the fifth line of each stanza:
   Let them *lie.* Suppose they *die?*
   The chance was they might take her eye.
[3] A few lyrics in *Pippa Passes* are strict octosyllabic couplets.
[4] For discussion of Duple-triple rhythm see Chapter XVII.

> With so unfeigned a gust—who knows if
> They did not prefer our friend to Joseph?   (237-8)

And not seldom they are triple:

> Than he handled it so, in fine irreverence,
> ⋯   ⋯   ⋯   ⋯
> And, in patchwork of chapters and texts in severence,
> (155,7)

They sometimes make good pentameters because the final word in the triple rhyme is too heavy to become subordinate:

> But so it is everywhere, one way with all of them!
> These people have really felt, no doubt,
> A something, the motion they style the Call of them;
> (239-41)

The other qualification that must be made is that *Christmas Eve* is not really in couplets, but is constantly varied by alternating and enclosing rhyme schemes. This is a typical passage: (aabbcdceedfggfhh)

> She too must stop, wring the poor ends dry
> Of a draggled shawl, and add thereby
> Her tribute to the door-mat, sopping
> Already from my own clothes' dropping,
> Which yet she seemed to grudge I should stand on:
>   Then, stooping down to take off her pattens,
> She bore defiantly, in each hand one,
> Planted together before her breast
> And its babe, as good as a lance in rest.
>   Close on her heels, the dingy satins
> Of a female something, past me flitted,
>   With lips as much too white, as a streak
>   Lay far too red on each hollow cheek;
> And it seemed the very door-hinge pitied
> All that was left of a woman once,
> Holding at least its tongue for the nonce.   (65-80)

The rhymes are not only widely separated but they are also imperfect: *stand on: hand one; flitted:pitied;*

once:nonce. These sections of the poem (and they predominate) do not produce the effect, certainly, of the regular octosyllabic couplets of *Easter Day,* and *The Italian in England.*

In contrast with the rhymes of the pentameter couplets, where they are so unobtrusive that the reader is not always conscious of them, the rhymes of the tetrameter couplets stand as conspicuous landmarks at the end of each line. They ring with regularity like the warning bell of a typewriter, and they will not be subordinated. They occur so often in the short lines that not even the high percentage of enjambment (47%) can subdue them as it can in the pentameters. On the contrary, the constant enjambment makes the short choppy octosyllables seem even shorter and choppier without effectively distracting attention away from the couplet rhymes. When the thought tries to soar out of its metrical restraint, it seems to be held back by a clipped wing. Lines frankly end-stopped are, to my ear, more pleasing than the jerky overflow of such passages as:

> —The skylark, taken by surprise
> As we ourselves, shall recognize
> Sudden the end. For suddenly
> It comes; the dreadfulness must be
> In that; all warrants the belief—
> 'At night it cometh like a thief.'
> *(Easter Day* 471-6)

and

> Death so nigh,
> When time must end, eternity
> Begin,—and cannot I compute,
> Weigh loss and gain together, suit
> My actions to the balance drawn,
> And give my body to be sawn
> Asunder, hacked in pieces, tied
> To horses, stoned, burned, crucified,
> Like any martyr of the list? *(Ibid.* 37-45)

Except for *Christmas Eve,* which is iambic-anapestic, Browning does not make any striking variations from the regular iambic of the traditional couplet. The most frequent, as the most to be expected, is the direct attack instead of the expected anacrusis:

> Leaving exposed the utmost walls   (*Easter Day* 544)

But, allowing for variations in readings, there are still less than 10 per cent of these beginnings.

Very rarely are the first two measures triple, and then the syllables flow into each other:

> "Such is man's usual gratitude,   (*Easter Day* 204*)*
> Find a live actual listener,   (355)
> Love survives in me, albeit those   (935)

Still more rarely is the third measure trisyllabic after the direct attack:

> Shuddered at,—all, the heavens grew black   (235)

The single triples are nearly all subject to the usual rules of elision, but they are none the less definite and pleasing variations from the expected rhythm.

> A fierce vindictive scribble of red   (511)
> How senses hornier than his hand   (446)
> Old memories to new dreams, nor scorn   (945)
> Then (sickening even while I spoke)   (890)

Weak or failing stresses are very common:

> And unevadable, the fact.   (555)
> Mere theories for blame or praise,   (392)
> Amid your veritable muck,   (307)
> With a mere probability,   (127)

Extra accents are rare, because the phrases more often support than conflict with the verse pattern:

> Briers, thistles, from our private plot,   (225)
> But there be certain words, broad, plain,   (257)
> 'Pinch your own arm, boy, and be sure   (500)
> Of that dry green old aqueduct   (*It. in Eng.* 7)

Monosyllabic measures seldom occur; when they do
it is usually in the first measure:

> And the | gay | heart be taught to ache,   (215)
> At | first | turn of the rusty key,

but occasionally in others:

> And judge if a | mere | foppery   (544)
> In the | same | place, with the | same | eyes:
>
> *(It. in Eng.* 89)

All of these variations are comparatively rare, however, and the prevailing tone of the couplets is one of
regularity and conformity.

> As I declare our Poet, him
> Whose insight makes all others dim:
> A thousand poets pried at life,
> And only one amid the strife
> Rose to be Shakespeare: (*Christmas Eve* 980-4)

Alexandrine Couplets

After the deadly experiment of Drayton's *Polyolbion*,
with its monotonous, gouty-footed couplets, the alexandrine was long out of favor and had to wait for
Browning for patronage of high order. It was used
as a variant line for other meters, but it was not considered a good medium for long poems. Browning,
with characteristic perversity, chose this traditionally
slow, lumbering couplet for *Fifine at the Fair* with all
its 2,355 lines. And with characteristic energy he made
the alexandrine beat its sleepy wings with some fervor
instead of allowing it to "drag its slow length along."

In part the animation of *Fifine* is due, of course, to
its lively subject matter and its sprightly monologue,
whereas the dullness of *Polyolbion* is as much in subject
matter as in metrical form; a dialogue between Wat-
ling Street and the Ver on the ruins of Verulam might
conceivably be dull even in trochaic tetrameter! But

Browning has been at some pains to avoid the snares which the alexandrine lays for the unwary, and this has made *Fifine* metrically interesting.

In the first place, it avoids the dignified slowness of the usual alexandrine.   In the very first lines it skips away with great energy of spirit:

> O trip and skip, Elvire!   Link arm in arm with me!
> Like husband and like wife, together let us see
> The tumbling-troop arrayed, the strollers on their stage,
> Drawn up and under arms, and ready to engage.

This vivacity, which fluctuates but never subsides, is in itself one worthy distinction of this poem.

It also avoids with considerable success the tendency of the six-measure line to fall exactly into two trimeters with a cesura after each, by a generous percentage of run on lines (34%), and by a skillful variation of the position of the cesura.   Short passages like the one just quoted, where the lines are end-stopped and bisected by the cesura, are relieved by passages like the following where the lines are enjambed and the cesura varied:

LXXXVI

> That's the first o' the truth found: all things, slow
> Or quick i' the passage, come at last to that, you know!
> Each has a false outside, whereby a truth is forced
> To issue from within: truth, falsehood, are divorced
> By the excepted eye, at the rare season, for
> The happy moment. Life means—learning to abhor
> The false, and love the true, truth treasured snatch by snatch,
> Waifs counted at their worth.   And when with strays they match
> I' the parti-colored world,—when, under foul, shines fair,
> And truth, displayed i' the point, flashes forth everywhere
> I' the circle, manifest to soul, though hid from sense,
> And no obstruction more affects this confidence,—
> When faith is ripe for sight,—why, reasonably, then
> Comes the great clearing-up.   Wait threescore years and ten!

Even though nine of these fourteen lines have a medial cesura, the effect of two trimeters is avoided by the enjambment and the varying position of the other cesuras. Thus, while 53 per cent of the lines of *Fifine* have cesuras after the sixth syllable, 15 per cent have cesuras after the fourth, 9 after the second, etc. To put it in the form of a table:

Percentage of lines with the cesura after syllables:

1	2	3	4	5	6	7	8	9	10	11
7%	9%	8%	15%	5%	53%	7%	7%	7%	5%	4%

Although the rhymes are always separated by enough syllables in such a long line to prevent clang, in these passages where enjambment is so frequent they are as silent as the rhymes of the pentameter couplets; and unless the reader was looking for them, I doubt if he was conscious of them when and if he read the foregoing passage.

Ivan Ivanovitch adds to these features of the six-measure couplet a great many triple measures; some passages are in fact duple-triple.

> "'Tis the regular pad of the wolves in pursuit of the
> life in the sledge!
> An army they are: close-packed they press like the
> thrust of a wedge:
> They increase as they hunt: for I see, through the
> pine-trunks ranged each side,
> Slip forth new fiend and fiend, make wider and still
> more wide
> The four-footed steady advance. The foremost—none
> may pass:
> They are elders and lead the line, eye and eye—
> green-glowing brass!
>
> (125-130)

By the sheer energy of his composition, and with the aid of these simple metrical devices, Browning was able to write nearly three thousand alexandrines without seriously offending good ears.

CHAPTER XV

TROCHAIC VERSE

Exactly what constitutes the difference, if any, between iambic and trochaic verse is warmly controversial. The question is complicated by the fact that the poets have always found it unobjectionable to shift from one to the other at will in the same poem. Half the lines of *L'Allegro* are iambic, and there are only nine trochaic lines in the last fifty. Milton writes:

> Such as hang on Hebe's cheek,
> And love to live in dimple sleek;
> Sport that wrinkled Care derides,
> And Laughter holding both his sides.   (29-32)

and Dyer:

> See on the Mountain's southern side,
> Where the Prospect opens wide,
> Where the Ev'ning gilds the Tide;
> How close and small the Hedges lie!
> *(Grongar Hill)*

So with all the eighteenth century octosyllables.

In practice, trochaic verse has been used in short lyrics in happy moods, and as a result there has grown up the metrical fiction that trochaic verse is lighter, gayer, more tripping than iambic because it is trochaic. But there is no difference in this respect between

> Sport that wrinkled Care derides,

and the following iambic line

> And laughter holding both his sides.

In Browning's *Song,* one line reads:

> Holds earth aught—speak truth—above her?

and seven lines farther on it reappears as:

> If earth holds aught—speak truth—above her?

Metrically the only difference is the preposition at the beginning.   Moreover, *One Word More* is trochaic and thoughtful, while *Memorabilia* is iambic and gay.

Theoretically, then, there is no difference, after the first accent marks off the beginning of the measure, whether we write:

> Pledged my soul to endless duty (*St. Martin's S.* 34)

or

> I pledged my soul to endless duty

But it is quite likely that the reader hears them in distinct patterns.

The real difference between the two exists chiefly in the mind of the reader.   For he attunes his ear differently for lines beginning with direct attack than for those having an anacrusis; and his anticipation seizes the words and throws them over a different pattern.   The ear tries to hear "dum-te, dum-te, dum-te," and it is this subjective anticipation which constitutes the chief difference between iambic and trochaic.   The expected pattern may be established so firmly that the ear is distinctly annoyed when it is compelled to readjust itself.   This happens in *St. Martin's Summer* where, after seven stanzas of regular trochaic lines, the pattern suddenly and without apparent reason shifts to iambic in the last ten.   But where the mixture of the two is a regular thing, as in *L'Allegro* and *Grongar Hill,* the ear quickly adjusts itself to the constant shift, as to a double anacrusis or direct attack in blank verse, and keeps its pattern flexible until it has tested the beginning of the line. The poets followed this principle when they constructed such poems.   Only when a prominent syllable stands at the beginning, as an anacrusis instead of an accent, will the ear be likely to err in attacking it; but if it does misjudge, it must make a new beginning.   It is always interesting to observe the reading of one not too familiar with a given poem in mixed metre.

The reader may or may not preserve his sense of trochaic movement as distinct from iambic through long lines of five, six, seven, or eight measures, depending upon the phrasing—whether it supports the pattern with such words as "happy," and "twinkle," or with strong direct attack and end-stopped lines with feminine ending—and upon the aggressiveness with which he anticipates and hears a given pattern.

Browning had an unusually strong sense for pattern, and it is plainly evident that he was aware of a distinct difference between an iambic and a trochaic pattern. Out of the twenty-two poems which may be called trochaic, in only five short ones are iambic and trochaic lines mixed. *The Boy and the Angel* begins trochaic, but the third line is iambic, and after the sixth line trochees are the exception (only sixteen in seventy-eight lines). In the *Song*, the first stanza is trochaic, the second iambic. *Before* has three iambic lines in forty. *Waring* mixes them at will. *St. Martin's Summer* has seven trochaic and ten iambic stanzas. The first line of *Humility* and of *Poetics* is iambic; all the rest are trochaic.

But the other seventeen poems, amounting to 2,325 lines, are trochaic without a single anacrusis to disturb the pattern; and four of these are long: *One Word More*, 201; *Clive*, 240; *Pietro of Abano*, 445; *La Saisiaz*, 618. Trochaic rhythm cannot be continuously sustained in this manner unless the poet himself keeps vividly in mind the trochaic pattern as he fashions his lines. The normal swing of English verse seems to be iambic, and trochaic verse is always threatening to shift over into that movement. When Browning, or any poet, preserves through several hundred lines an unbroken trochaic pattern, there is nothing more certain than that he has consciously taken pains to preserve a pattern which he feels to be different from iambic.

Some of Browning's most distinctive effects are achieved by combining short trochaic lines of two, three, and four measures. One of the most unusual of these is *In a Year,* with the combination 3242.[1] The arrangement 334442 occurs in *St. Martin's Summer;*[2] 3232 in *A Woman's Last Word;*[3] 3343 with feminine endings in *Flute Music.*[4] *Humility, A Serenade at the Villa, At the "Mermaid," Soliloquy of the Spanish Cloister,* are Browning's examples of the familiar tetrameter lines. The last one is unique in its colloquial phrase conflicts and monkish oaths which strain the pattern; the others carefully preserve it by avoiding conflict, weak stresses, and enjambment. *Cristina and Monaldeschi* is also tetrameter but it has the peculiar rhyme scheme abbbaccc. The other trochaic poems are in lines of more than four measures. These have attracted considerable attention because, previous to Tennyson and Browning, trochaic verse was generally confined to short lines. Browning experimented with lines of five, six, seven, and eight measures.

One Word More is the most remarkable of this group.[5] The lines, as in all Browning's trochaic verse, are extremely regular with very little variation. Only two lines in the entire poem break the pattern; line 30

---

[1] Quoted page 128. It is desperately futile to identify this metre with a meaningless arrangement of the Quadrupedante line of the *Aeneid,* as Thomson does in *The Rhythm of Speech,* p. 329, or to make an abstruse metrical problem of this simple but exquisite combination of short lines which Browning loved.

[2] Quoted page 125.

[3] Quoted page 117.

[4] Quoted page 131.

[5] Dr. Andrews has discussed this poem quite fully and admirably in *The Writing and Reading of Verse,* pp. 270-271.

Cried, and the world cried too, "Ours, the treasure!"

where the phrasing makes the first measure triple, and line 37

When, his left-hand i' the hair o' the wicked.

where his fondness for apostrophes betrays him into a bad line. Each line begins with an accent, and ends with a light ending to preserve the trochaic effect to the end. Light stresses are rare and continuously varied, and each line ends with a completed phrase or sentence.

There they are, my fifty men and women
Naming me the fifty poems finished!
Take them, Love, the book and me together:
Where the heart lies, let the brain lie also.

Here are trochaic lines with the dignified seriousness of iambic pentameter. The metrical art lies pretty largely in the strong, unfailing direct attack at the beginning of each line and the absence of enjambment; without these buttresses the rhythm would probably lose its individuality when read in paragraphs.

In *Fears and Scruples* (the other poem in pentameter) every other line has a feminine ending, each line begins with a heavy stress, the phrases support the movement even though they are short and are uttered in monologue. The stanzas are quatrains with alternate rhyme.

"Letters?" (hear them!) "You a judge of writing?
Ask the experts! How they shake the head
O'er these characters, your friend's inditing—
Call them forgery from A to Z!

Trochaic hexameters are brittle and break regularly into two trimeters. In *Before* the cesura usually occurs after the unstressed sixth syllable, the new beginning in the middle of the line reinforcing the trochaic movement.

> God must judge the couple: ‖ leave them as they are (2)
> Strike no arm out further, ‖ stick and stink as now, (6)
> Let him pace at pleasure, ‖ past the walls of rose, (17)
> So much for the culprit. ‖ Who's the martyred man? (25)

If the sixth syllable is an important monosyllable, the line tends to lengthen into seven measures:

> Let them fight it out, friend! things have gone too far. (1)
> Why, you would not bid men, sunk in such a slough,   (5)
> Better sin the whole sin, sure that God observes;   (13)

This almost inevitable tendency of the hexameter to break in the middle is also shown in the poems where it alternates with a seven-measure line. But the septenary shows an equally natural tendency to fall into four-four time, and the combination can be very pleasing. It occurs in *Poetics, Epilogue to Ferishtah's Fancies,* and *Magical Nature.*

> You, forsooth, a flower? ‖ Nay, my love, a jewel—
> | Jewel at no | mercy of a | moment in your | prime!
> | Time may fray the | flower-face: | kind be time or | cruel,
>   Jewel, from each facet, ‖ flash your laugh at time!
> *(Magical Nature)*

In *Pietro of Abano,* Browning tells a long story in trochaic verse using the combination 686768867. The eight-measure lines of *La Saisaiz* and *Clive* cannot stand erect; their excessive length always causes them to break at one of the joints, or the light stresses trip them into four-four time. But what can be done in way of phrasing and varying the cesura to preserve the integrity of the line, Browning has done.[6]

---

[6] For discussion and examples see pages 26-27.

CHAPTER XVI

THE TRIPLE RHYTHMS

Anapestic Movement

The number of poems in purely anapestic movement is comparatively small in Browning,[1] although the combined iambic-anapestic or duple-triple movement is, as we shall see, very common. This is due, at least in no small degree, to the fact that the language is prevailingly duple in the natural rhythm of its phrases; and if the anapestic pattern is strictly to be preserved, the phrases must often be forced into conformity. The result is likely to produce monotony.

The triple rhythms, whether dactylic or anapestic, have more go and more energy than duple rhythms because the proportion of unstressed syllables is larger, and the time value of each is correspondingly shorter. These two lines will be read in approximately, if not exactly the same time (three-four):

How soon a smile of God can change the world!

(*Balcony* 597)

All the breath and the bloom of the year in the bag of one bee:

(*Summum Bonum* 1)

but the first is calm and deliberate, and the second is hurried and breathless.

Because of the speed which it develops, the anapestic movement has always been found suitable for verse

---

[1] Triple movement shifts easily from anapestic to dactylic, and either in its purity is not very common. *The Laboratory* wavers between the two; *Apollo and the Fates* and *Fust and His Friends* have many dactylic lines; while *The Glove* begins and continues for eighteen lines as dactylic; not until line 26 is there a double anacrusis; all the endings are feminine except lines 123-156.

full of action and motion, where thought is less important than the sensation of speed. It is therefore especially appropriate for rapid narrative verse like *The Glove,* "*How They Brought the Good News from Ghent to Aix*," *Muckle-Mouth Meg,* and some parts of *The Flight of the Duchess.*

Browning has also used this movement for verse whose mood is one of calm reflection. But it is difficult to prevent this galloping anapestic steed from running away with the thought. Even in *Saul,* where the thought is more important than the metre, the rush of the anapests is often so breathless and consuming that the metre attracts the attention away from the meaning. After the swing of the metre has exhausted itself at the end of the line, the reader must often go back to see what has become of the meaning he has left behind. It is therefore an open question whether anapestic rhythm is suited for reflective poems.

But there is no open question about *The Glove,* or *Muckle-Mouth Meg,* or "*How They Brought the Good News.*" Here we want all the speed and go possible, for the mind is centered on the rush of events. "*How They Brought the Good News*" is the fastest of the group, due in part to the heated action which spurs it on, and in part to the clipped amphibrach phrases of:

> I sprang to the stirrup, and Joris, and he;
> I galloped, Dirck galloped, we galloped all three;
> "Good speed!" cried the watch, as the gate-bolts undrew;
> "Speed!" echoed the wall to us galloping through;
> Behind shut the postern, the lights sank to rest,
> And into the midnight we galloped abreast.

Browning's anapestic lines vary in length from dimeter to pentameter, but most of them are either trimeter or tetrameter. The trimeter is a heavier line in triple rhythm than in duple, of course, since it has eight or nine syllables which give enough volume for stability and enough length to carry the narrative with ease. *The Glove* is a good example of the adequacy of anapestic trimeter:

> The sentence no sooner was uttered,
> Than over the rails a glove fluttered,
> Fell close to the lion, and rested:
> The dame 'twas, who flung it and jested
> With life so, De Lorge has been wooing
> For months past; he sat there pursuing
> His suit, weighing out with nonchalance
> Fine speeches like gold from a balance.   (83-90)

The tetrameter line, with its twelve or thirteen syllables, is bound and held together by the anapestic movement. The strong tendency of tetrameters to break in the middle is not nearly so noticeable here. The reader is hardly conscious of the fact that exactly half of the lines in *"How They Brought the Good News"* are broken in the middle by a cesura, or that the other half have slight, unpunctuated cesuras near the middle of the line:

> Not a word to each other; ‖ we kept the great pace
> Neck by neck, stride by stride, ‖ never changing our place;
> I turned in my saddle | and made its girths tight,
> Then shortened each stirrup, ‖ and set the pique right,
> Rebuckled the check-strap, ‖ chained slacker the bit,
> Nor galloped less steadily Roland a whit.
>
> *(Stanza II)*

None of Browning's anapestic poems has more than five measures, and *Saul* is in fact the only poem that is pentameter.[2] Lines of greater length, like the hexameters of Swinburne's *Hymn to Proserpine,* and the septenaries of his *Hesperia,* are usually broken in spite of the impetuous rhythm. Even the pentameters are constantly subject to this bisection into two short

---

[2] A few lines in *Summum Bonum* are pentameter.

lines, the cesura after the eighth syllable breaking the five measures into a trimeter and a dimeter. It is a regular occurrence in *Saul*.

III

|| Then I, as was meet,
Knelt down to the God of my fathers, || and rose on my feet,
And ran o'er the sand burnt to powder. || The tent was unlooped;
I pulled up the spear that obstructed, || and under I stooped;
Hands and knees on the slippery grass-patch, || all withered
      and gone,
That extends to the second enclosure, || I groped my way on
Till I felt where the foldskirts fly open. || . . . etc., etc.

Browning must have recognized this tendency, for *The Englishman in Italy*, which in metre is exactly like *Saul*, is printed as two lines—a trimeter and a dimeter broken as those just quoted from *Saul*.[3] Several other poems recognize this cleavage and use it as the basis for new effects. *After*, for example, breaks up into a trimeter and a dimeter with couplet rhymes, as if *Saul* had an internal rhyme; but in the break-up a new form has evolved:[4]

Take the cloak from his face, and at first
      Let the corpse do its worst!
How he lies in his rights of a man!
      Death has done all death can.

Instans Tyrannus uses the same scheme, but varies it slightly by omitting a syllable from the anacrusis of the dimeter:

I

Of the million or two, more or less,
      I rule and possess,
One man, for some cause undefined,
      Was least to my mind.

In the later lines, however, the dimeter has a double anacrusis. Still another variation occurs in *James*

---

[3] See pages 137-8.

[4] The couplet rhyme gives the dimeter a distinct individuality, and the pair of lines does not exactly equal one line of *Saul*, as Hodgson contended it did in *Outcast Essays and Verse Translations*, p. 287.

Lee's Wife III, where the fifth measure is made into a separate line on alternate rhymes:

> The swallow has set her six young on the rail,
>   And looks seaward:
> And water's in stripes like a snake, olive-pale
>   To the leeward,—

All these poems, it will be noted, have a delicate interplay between the natural prose rhythm of the phrases and the anapestic verse pattern; they are neither monotonous nor disturbing. In *After,* only one line is at all doubtful:

> I stand here now, he lies in his place:
>   Cover the face!   (17-18)

The pattern is often further aided by alliterative phrases which reinforce the anapestic rhythm. They recall Swinburne:

All the *b*reath and the *b*loom of the year in the *b*ag of one *b*ee:
All the *w*onder and *w*ealth of the *m*ine in the heart of one *g*em:
In the core of one pearl all the *s*hade and the *s*hine of the *s*ea:
> *(Summum Bonum)*

*S*ound flesh and *s*ane soul in coherence, born *w*ealthy,
    Nay, *w*ise—how he *w*asted en*d*owment *d*esigned
For the *g*lory of *G*od and the *g*ood of mankind!
> *(Fust and His Friends* 143-5)

Bids *p*ause at no *p*art but *p*ress on, reach the whole.
For *p*etty and *p*oor is the *p*art ye envisage
> *(Apollo and the Fates* 190-1)

Behold you enshrined in these *b*looms of your *b*ringing,
These fruits of your *b*earing—nay, *b*irds of your *w*inging!
> *(Natural Magic* 16-17)

Saul stands, in line length, mood, and phrase conflict, as a unique experiment among Browning's anapests. The long lines of fourteen or fifteen syllables tend to break, as we have seen, after the third stress; although the impetuosity of the movement does help to hold them together. But the entire poem is

full of struggle: the metre strives with the thought
for the reader's attention, and the prose rhythm of
the phrases struggles against the rigid confines of the
verse pattern.   Sometimes the metre dominates and
runs away with the thought, as in some of the passages of close reasoning in section XVII:

The man taught enough, by life's dream, of the rest to make
    sure;
By the pain-throb, triumphantly winning intensified bliss,
And the next world's reward and repose, by the struggles in
    this.

Sometimes the two blend into each other, as in section
IX, where the anapests beat in tune with the passionate joy of life:

"Oh, our manhood's prime vigor!   No spirit feels waste,
Not a muscle is stopped in its playing nor sinew unbraced.
Oh, the wild joys of living! the leaping from rock up to rock,
The strong rending of boughs from the fir-tree, the cool silver
    shock
Of the plunge in the pool's living water, . . .   (68-72)

But sometimes the thought so completely dominates
the rhythm, and the prose phrases are so unhappy in
the verse pattern, that the whole structure all but falls
to pieces on the unwary reader who has not arbitrarily
marked off the temporal pattern beforehand.   This is
so obvious that it is almost an impertinence to cite
examples; for every reader of the poem has experienced the difficulty of such lines as,

And lo, with the leap of my spirit,—heart, hand, harp and voice.
Then I tuned my harp,—took off the lilies we twine round its
    chords
What was gone, what remained?   All to traverse 'twixt hope
    and despair,
Death was past, life not come: so he waited.
These good things being given, to go on, and give one more,
    the best?

Dactylic Movement

Dactyls, like trochees, are most successful in short lines. Although other poets (notably Longfellow) have lengthened them into hexameter and even octameter, Browning limits them to lines of from two to four measures. But even in short lines it is difficult to preserve the integrity of the movement. *Another Way of Love*, for example, begins favorably in dactylic movement, but it weakens in the second line, capitulates in the third, makes a feeble counter-attack in the ninth, and succumbs again in the tenth and eleventh.

> June was not over
> Though past the full,
> And the best of her roses
> Had yet to blow,
> When a man I know
> (But shall not discover,
> Since ears are dull,
> And time discloses)
> Turned him and said with a man's true air,
> Half sighing a smile in a yawn, as 't were,—
> "If I tire of your June, will she greatly care?"

The phrasing of the second stanza, however, with its direct attack and its double and triple rhymes, braces the movement so rigidly that only a single line of the dimeters surrenders.

> Well, dear, in-*doors with you!*
> True! serene deadness
> Tries a man's temper.
> What's in the blossom
> June wears on her bosom?
> Can it clear *scores with you?*
> Sweetness and redness,
> *Eadem semper!*

These ingenious triple rhymes, although they bolster up the dactylic movement, are impossible for a whole

poem; and when used too often, as in *Pacchiarotto,*
they are like to become ludicrous. Browning uses
them occasionally in his serious dactylic verse, as:
*doors with you: scores with you; ball of it: all of it;
rearranging it : changing it;* but for the most part he
frankly uses masculine and feminine endings. The
two-measure lines of *Pisgah-Sights* and *Love,* with
their feminine endings, become therefore a series of
adonics.

> So, the year's done with!
> *(Love me forever!)*
> All March begun with,
> April's endeavor;
> **May**-wreaths that bound me
> June needs must sever;
> Now snows fall round me,
> Quenching June's fever—
> *(Love me forever!)*
>
> *(Love)*

No better examples of the effect of phrasing upon
movement could be brought together than the dactylic
trimeters and tetrameters of *Misconceptions* and *Master Hugues of Saxe-Gotha.* For in *Misconceptions* the
phrases and the metrical pattern support each other
like David and Jonathan; while in *Master Hugues of
Saxe-Gotha* they are as antagonistic as Samuel and
Saul. In *Misconceptions* the movement is easy, natural, and unmistakable:

> This is the spray the Bird clung to,
> Making it blossom with pleasure,
> Ere the high tree-top she sprung to,
> Fit for her nest and her treasure.
> Oh, what a hope beyond measure
> Was the poor spray's, which the flying feet hung to,—
> So to be singled out, built in, and sung to!

But if the reader does not get the rhythm of *Master
Hugues* beating strongly in his ear before he gives at-

tention to the words, he is likely to have a fall before he gets far. The metrical pattern is superimposed upon the resisting phrases:

> One dissertates, he is candid;
>> Two must discept,—has distinguished;
> Three helps the couple, if ever yet man did;
>> Four protests; Five makes a dart at the thing wished:
> Back to One, goes the case bandied.   (Stanza 14)

If these two poems represent the extremes in phrasing, *The Lost Leader* and *Holy-Cross Day* [5] show the possible extremes in mood, and the effect of the cesura in four-measure dactylic lines. In the jocular *Holy-Cross Day* the cesura occurs in the middle, breaking the line regularly into two dimeters:

> Higgledy piggledy, packed we lie,
> Rats in a hamper, swine in a sty,
> Wasps in a bottle, frogs in a sieve,
> Worms in a carcass, fleas in a sleeve.
> Hist! square shoulders, settle your thumbs
> And buzz for the bishop—here he comes.

In *The Lost Leader,* also in tetrameter, the internal pause is more skillfully varied. Lines which move spiritedly without interruption are intermixed with those broken by a cesura:

> Just for a handful of silver he left us,
>> Just for a riband to stick in his coat—
> Found the one gift of which fortune bereft us,
>> Lost all the others she lets us devote;
> They, with the gold to give, || doled him out silver,
>> So much was theirs who so little allowed:
> How all our copper had gone for his service!
>> Rags—were they purple, || his heart had been proud!
> We that had loved him so, || followed him, honored him,
>> Lived in his mild and magnificent eye,

[5] Many of the lines in the last half of this poem are anapestic.

Learned his great language, || caught his clear accents,
  Made him our pattern to live and to die!
Shakespeare was of us, || Milton was for us,
  Burns, Shelley, were with us,— || they watch from their
    graves!
He alone breaks from the van and the freemen,
  —He alone sinks to the rear and the slaves!

The medial cesura falls after the sixth syllable in the
fifth line; after the fifth in the eighth line; after the
sixth in the ninth; after the fifth in the eleventh and
thirteenth lines, where a rest displaces a syllable; and
after the sixth in the fourteenth line, the only one
beginning with an anacrusis.

The Cavalier Tunes [6] show the movement in its dash-
ing, high-spirited mood, full of gay energy. The rapid
movement which the large proportion of unaccented
syllables can give it, makes it preeminently suited for
these brave songs. The few lines with anacrusis re-
lieve rather than upset the prevailingly dactylic movement:

Hampden to hell, and his obsequies' knell.
Serve Hazelrig, Fiennes, and young Harry as well!
England, good cheer!   Rupert is near!
Kentish and loyalists, keep we not here,
  Chorus.—Marching along, fifty-score strong,
    Great-hearted gentlemen, singing this song?

[6] See also Chapter XIII, p. 134.

CHAPTER XVII

DUPLE-TRIPLE MOVEMENT

DUPLE-TRIPLE movement is a free combination of iambic-anapestic or trochaic-dactylic measures in the same line, but is neither duple nor triple in its effect over a group of lines. It is not exactly "trisyllabic substitution," as it has been called, because there is no duple norm from which the triples are felt to vary, as there is, for example, in blank verse. When, in a pattern of iambic pentameter, the reader comes full upon the line

Like the skipping of rabbits by moonlight,—three slim shapes,
(*Fra Lippo* 59)

he is astonished because his ear has been accustomed to expect duple rhythm. But when he comes upon this from *Evelyn Hope*

There was place and to spare for the frank young smile, (51)

he is not even mildly surprised because the first few lines led him to expect triple measures as a part of the verse pattern. The triples are as much a part of the movement as the duples, and they are so inseparable that they must be regarded as forming a distinct movement.

Duple-triple movement was first brought to critical attention by Coleridge's *Christabel* with its preface on the "new principle" of its metre. In comparison with the more highly developed form in Browning's fifty poems, however, *Christabel* is not in the strictest sense duple-triple. For the triples in *Christabel* are inserted by design as an "occasional variation in number of syllables . . . in correspondence with some transition,

in the nature of the imagery or passion." The reader
never forgets that the norm is duple; after each de-
parture the duple reasserts itself. Lines 30-48, for
example, are regularly duple; lines 49-58 are varied
with triples; but lines 58 ff. again become duple. In
Browning there are no such passages where one type
excludes the other; [1] practically every line has at least
one measure of each, and the reader never considers
either the duple or the triple as the normal from which
the other is an "occasional variation." But *Christabel*
did call attention back to the fact that the two could
be mixed in the same line without violating the temporal equality of the measures; that the four accents
of the lines mark off the same time without regard to
the number of syllables.

<blockquote>
She | kneels be | neath the | huge oak | tree
On the | topmost | twig that looks | up at the | sky.
</blockquote>

The free combination of duples and triples creates
a variety of rhythms of great beauty. Some of Browning's best remembered poems are in this movement:
*Evelyn Hope; Home Thoughts, from Abroad; Life in
a Love; My Star; Old Pictures in Florence; The Statue
and the Bust; Up at a Villa—Down in the City*, etc.,
etc. Its highest virtue is perhaps that it escapes the
monotony of a rigid pattern without becoming lawless
or unmusical; and it utilizes the natural rhythm of the
prose phrases without excessive conflict or tedious
regularity. The movement of *Up at a Villa—Down in
the City* is remarkably like talk, considering its hexameters and its tercet stanza form:

Had I but plenty of money, money enough and to spare,
The house for me, no doubt, were a house in the city-square;
Ah, such a life, such a life, as one leads at the window there!

---

[1] Excepting *Christmas Eve*, the characteristics of which we have already
noted.

Something to see, by Bacchus, something to hear, at least!
There, the whole day long, one's life is a perfect feast;
While up at a villa one lives, I maintain it, no more than a
    beast.

The short lines of *Confessions* approach even more nearly the rhythm of speech:

What is he buzzing in my ears?
  "Now that I come to die,
Do I view the world as a vale of tears?"
  Ah, reverend sir, not I!

Of course Browning does not entirely avoid conflict between the phrases and the verse pattern, even when it is as natural in its rhythm and as elastic in its pattern as duple-triple. But the difficulty of parts of *Saul* or of *Master Hugues of Saxe-Gotha* is not felt even amid the apparent roughness of:

For—see your cellerage!
  There are four big butts of Milton's brew.
How comes it you make old drips and drops
Do duty, and there devotion stops?
Leave such an abyss of malt and hops
  Embellied in butts which bungs still glue?
You hate your bard! A fig for your rage!
  Free him from cellerage!
      (*Epilogue to Pacchiarotto* Stanza XII)

The range of the poems in duple-triple rhythm in stanza form and line length is extremely wide. There are the short dimeters of *James Lee's Wife I,* which are as much duple-triple in their effect as longer lines:[2]

Thou art a man,
  But I am thy love,
For the lake, its swan;
  For the dell its dove:
And for thee—(oh, haste!)
  Me, to bend above,
Me, to hold embraced.

---

[2] The first eight lines of *My Star* are in the same metre.

There are many trimeters, like these from *Reverie:*

> Through the barrier of flesh, till keen
> She climbs from the calm and clear,
> Through turbity all between,
> From the known to the unknown here,
> Heaven's "Shall be," from Earth's "Has been"?
>   (Stanza 40)

There are many tetrameters like these of *Parting at Morning:*

> Round the cape of a sudden came the sea,
> And the sun looked over the mountain's rim:
> And straight was a path of gold for him,
> And the need of a world of men for me.

There are combined trimeters and tetrameters:

> "That psalm," the Professor smiled, "shall be
> Untroubled by doubt which dirtieth
> Pellucid streams when an ass like thee
> Would drink there—the Nine-and-thirtieth.
>   (*Pambo* 13-16)

There are combined tetrameters, trimeters, and dimeters of *James Lee's Wife V:*

> On the turf, sprang gay
> With his films of blue,
> No cricket, I'll say,
> But a warhorse, barded and chanfroned too,
> The gift of a quixote-mage to his knight,
> Real fairy, with wings all right.

There are the hexameters of *Up at a Villa—Down in the City.* And there are the septenaries of *Martin Relph:*

If I last as long as Methuselah I shall never forgive myself:
But—God forgive me, that I pray, unhappy Martin Relph,
As coward, coward I call him—him, yes, him! Away from me!
Get you behind the man I am now, you man that I used to be!

The distribution of the duples and triples is governed by no fixed law. The *Flower's Name,* for example, which is prevailingly trochaic-dactylic, has thirty-two lines with direct attack, thirteen with an anacrusis, and three with double anacrusis. But the second stanza has but two direct-attack lines, while the last one has eight. Each line of the poem has at least one triple, but twenty-two have only one, and two lines are entirely triple. The following notation will show at a glance the difference in the structure of stanzas two and six.

		(2)					(6)		
	xx	xxx	xx	x		xxx	xx	xx	xx
x	xxx	xx	xx	x		xxx	xxx	xx	x
x	xx	xxx	xx	x		xxx	xxx	xxx	xx
x	xxx	xxx	xx	x		xx	xxx	xxx	x
	xx	xxx	xx	x		xx	xxx	xxx	xx
xx	xx	xxx	xx	x		xxx	xx	xxx	x
x	xx	xx	xxx	x		xxx	xx	xxx	xx
x	xx	xxx	xx	x		xxx	xxx	xxx	x

CHAPTER XVIII

IMITATIONS OF CLASSICAL METRES

BROWNING'S imitations of classical hexameters in *Pheidippides* and *Ixion,* following the laws of English rather than Greek or Latin verse, are evidently intended to be accentual and not quantitative. But, as Thompson well says,[1] "We can see . . . how dangerous is the ground and how elusive the subject matter, when we generalize and talk of one national verse as quantitative, of another as accentual, and yet another as syllabic." *Pheidippides* is an imitation of the Greek dactylic hexameter; or in English terms, six-measure lines in falling duple-triple rhythm, since the spondee of the classics is a duple in English. Unlike the Homeric hexameter, *Pheidippides* never ends with a spondee or a feminine ending; except for this the Homeric hexameters which Coleridge translated from Schiller would fit into it:

| Strongly it | bears us a | long in | swelling and |
  limitless | billows,   *(Coleridge)*

| That sent a | blaze through my | blood; off | off and a |
  way was I | back,   *(Phei.* 42)

| Nothing be | fore and | nothing be | hind but the |
  sky and the | ocean.   *(Coleridge)*

| Have ye kept | faith, proved | mindful of | honors we |
  paid you ere | while?   *(Phei.* 46)

Through the first five measures, *Pheidippides* holds to the classical scheme in which the first four may be either dactyls or spondees but the fifth must normally be a dactyl. The sixth measure omits a final syllable.

[1] William Thomson, *The Rhythm of Speech,* p. 314.

This poem is further distinguished by its short adonic and choriambic phrases,[2] regularly marked off by commas. In some lines the adonics predominate:

> First I salute this | soil of the blessed, | river and rock!
> Gods of my birthplace, | daemons and heroes, | honor to all!
>   (1-2)
> Archons of Athens, | topped by the tettix, | see, I return!
>   (9)
> Crowned with the myrtle, | did you command me, | Athens
>   and you,   (11)

In other lines the choriambic phrasing prevails, with a rest taking the place of the final syllable in the adonic. The last line of nearly every stanza has these measures.

> Present to help, || potent to save, | Pan—patron I call! (8)
> Over the hills, || under the dales, | down pits and up
>   peaks.   (16)
> "Persia has come, || Athens asks aid, | and still they
>   debate?   (30)
> Athens must wait, || patient as we— | who judgment
>   suspend."   (40)
> "Athens, she only, | rears me no fane, || makes me no
>   feast!   (73)

The time is clearly three-four in all these lines; and occasionally the entire line swings smoothly to its end in triple rhythm:

> Gravely they turned to take counsel, to cast for ex-
>   cuses. I stood
> Quivering,—the limbs of me fretting as fire frets, an
>   inch from dry wood: (28-29)

One group of lines has a full extra measure making them septenaries:

> —but Athens, shall Athens sink,
>
>   ′   ′   ′   ′   ′   ′   ′
> Drop into dust and die—the flower of Hellas utterly die,

---

[2] This has led Omond to call it "choriambic" metre. (T. S. Omond: *A Study of Metre*, p. 149.) As a matter of fact, the adonic phrases are as numerous as the choriambic.

Díe, with the wíde world spítting at Spárta, the stúpid,

the stánder-bý?

Ánswer me quíck, what hélp, what hánd do you strétch o'er

destrúction's brínk?   (19-22)

There is in fact such constant variation throughout
the entire poem that few successive lines are exactly
alike. The whole arrangement, with the dominant
adonic and choriambic phrases, gives it the effect of
breathlessness and makes it as well suited to the
broken speech of the exhausted runner as the arrangement of *"How They Brought the Good News From
Ghent to Aix"* is to the gallop of horses.

Ixion is modeled on the elegiac metre of the ancients,
usually defined as a dactylic hexameter alternating
with a dactylic pentameter. But in English prosody,
certainly, this so-called "pentameter" has six time
parts, the third being normally a monosyllable and a
rest, as in Coleridge's oft-quoted English example of
this metre:

| In the hex | ameter | rises the | fountains | silvery | column;
| In the pen | tameter | ay ^ | falling in | melody | back.

Ixion follows the scheme of these lines. It has no
rhymes and no stanzas. Every other line beginning
with the first has a feminine ending; and every other
one beginning with the second has (with a few exceptions) a monosyllabic third measure. The first few
lines establish the pattern from which there are no
striking variations:

High in the dome, suspended, of Hell, sad triumph, behold us!
    Here the revenge of a God, there the amends of a Man.
Whirling forever in torment, flesh once mortal, immortal
    Made—for a purpose of hate—able to die and revive,

Pays to the uttermost pang, then, newly for payment replen-
    ished,
    Doles out—old yet young—agonies ever afresh;
Whence the result above me: torment is bridged by a rainbow,—
    Tears, sweat, blood,—each spasm, ghastly once, glorified
    now.

Abt Vogler begins as if it too were following the
elegiac scheme with its alternating hexameter and
"pentameter" lines. Except for the truncation of the
final syllable in the hexameter, and the division into
stanzas with rhyme, the first lines of *Abt Vogler* are
like those of *Ixion:*

Would that the structure brave, the manifold music I build,
    Bidding my organ obey, calling its keys to their work,
Claiming each slave of the sound, at a touch, as when Solomon
    willed
    Armies of angels that soar, legions of demons that lurk,

But this elegiac form is not continued with any strict-
ness; the fifth line has the monosyllabic measure
instead of the sixth, while the seventh and eighth each
has an anacrusis:

| Man, brute, | reptile, | fly,— | alien of | end and of | aim,
    | Adverse, | each from the | other heaven— | high, hell— | deep
    re | moved,—
Should | rush into | sight at | once as he | named the in | effable |
    Name,
    And | pile him a | palace | straight, to | pleasure the | princess
    he | loved!

Browning seems to forget the classical model as the
poem proceeds; the second stanza recovers the tune
for a few lines but loses it again. From this point on
it becomes increasingly apparent that the poem is actually in duple-triple rhythm with either rising or
falling movement with only an occasional echo of the
elegiac model. The total effect of the poem is more
native than classical.

Prospice is also haunted by the ghost of classical hexameters or anapests (since the hexameter has no up-beat). This line

Fear | death?—to | feel the | fog in my | throat, the | mist in my | face,

is exactly like some of the lines in *Pheidippides,*

When | Persia—so | much as | strews not the | soil—is | cast in the | sea,   (78)

But it is not classical; it makes a new pattern by breaking up the duple-triple hexameter into a tetrameter and a dimeter with alternate rhyme and rising movement:

> Fear death?—to feel the fog in my throat,
>   The mist in my face,
> When the snows begin, and the blasts denote
>   I am nearing the place,

The interesting attempt which Thomson has made to identify the metre of *In a Year* with the "Quadrupedante" line of the *Aeneid,*[3] *Through the Metidja to Abd-el-Kadr* with the greater ionic,[4] and *A Pretty Woman* with the lesser ionic,[5] leaves us quite unmoved except for a certain sympathy for the desperateness of the attempt. It ignores Browning's love of short lines and thereby makes a mountain of a very small mole-hill. *In A Year* is a typical Browning combination of dimeter, trimeter, and tetrameter on a complex rhyme scheme. To break the eight-line stanza in the middle, put the separate lines into one, then add two syllables to the Quadrupedante line which destroy its meaning, lop off the final syllable, "add a little tripletic decoration," allow for a little roughness in the reading, and behold they are alike! is to end in the mare's nest which Thomson suspects.

[3] *The Rhythm of Speech,* pp. 328-331. *Aeneid* VIII. 596.
[4] *Ibid.* pp. 343-345.
[5] *Ibid.* pp. 345-346.

But the analogy between *Give a Rouse* and Tyrtaeus'
fragment of a war song seems less violent. Read side
by side it is true that ". . . this unmatched—shall we
say matchless?—cavalier tune of Browning's is an
almost exact replica of the movement of the oldest
war-song extant, as interpreted in his day. If the
Greek lyric did not rap out the last two syllables with
the soldierly vigor of the English one, it possessed a
feature that may have been in its favor as a marching
song, but certainly it missed the chance of 'giving a
rouse,' which a lucky error enabled Browning to seize.
. . . Browning seizes precisely that abruptness and
those consonantal rudenesses which are scrupulously
avoided in the Greek." [6]

This is the fragment:

ἄγετ' ὦ Σπάρτας εὐάνδρου
κοῦροι πατέρων πολιατᾶν
λαιᾷ μὲν ἴτυν προβάλεσθε
δόρυ δ' εὐτόλμως
μὴ φειδόμενοι τᾶς ζωᾶς
οὐ γὰρ πάτριον τᾷ Σπάρτᾳ.

[6] *Ibid.* pp. 332-333.

CHAPTER XIX

VERSE IN FOUR-FOUR TIME

(Quadruple or Dipodic Measures)

VERSE IN FOUR-FOUR time or quadruple rhythm has as a norm a measure of four syllables. It differs from ordinary iambic or trochaic rhythm in that it is felt in time units of four syllables instead of two because the third syllable of each measure carries a stress distinctly lighter than the first. The heavy stresses falling upon the first, fifth, ninth (etc.) syllables establish the four syllable time grouping.

>   ′   ′   ′   ′
> | Savage I was | sitting in my | house, late | lone
> > *(Epilogue to Fifine* 1)

Once the movement is established, it moves with an irresistible swing; and the expectancy it incites in aggressive ears is strong enough to subordinate any conflicting prose rhythm of the phrases.

Obviously, verse in four-four time demands a wider sweep than verse in three-four time, or duple and triple rhythms; it usually requires at least three measures, more often four, making lines of twelve or more syllables.

Browning was fond enough of this rhythm to use it (with variations) in ten poems. One might, indeed, include *La Saisiaz* and say eleven, because its long lines (like those in *Locksley Hall*), fall continuously and easily into quadruple measures.

Petty feat and yet prodigious: every side my glance was bent
O'er the grandeur and the beauty lavished through the whole
   ascent.

181

Ledge by ledge, out broke new marvels, now minute and now
    immense:
Earth's most exquisite disclosure, heaven's own God in evidence!
                                    (3-6)

The rhythm may be either rising or falling, in various line-lengths and with many variations from the anticipated normal measure. In *A Toccata of Galuppi's* the rhythm is established in the first verse and continues quite regularly save for a few phrase conflicts.

Oh Gal | uppi, Baldas | sare, this is | very sad to | find!
I can | hardly miscon | ceive you; it would | prove me deaf and
    | blind;
But al | though I take your | meaning, 't is with | such a heavy |
        mind!
                                   (Stanza I.)

The insistence of this rhythm soon becomes strong enough to reduce all the lines to its pattern, rather joyfully sweeping through such stanzas as,

"Were you | happy?"—"Yes."—"And | are you still as | happy?"
    —"Yes, and | you?"
—"Then, more | kisses!"—"Did *I* | stop them when a | million
    seemed so | few?"
Hark, the | dominant's per | sistence till it | must be
    answered | to!

Home Thoughts, From the Sea, and Mertoun's Song in *A Blot in the 'Scutcheon,* Act I, have the same rhythm and line-length as *A Toccata of Galuppi's:*

There's a | woman like a | dew-drop, she's so | purer than
    the | purest;
And her | noble heart's the | noblest, yes, and | her sure
    faith's the | surest:
And her | eyes are dark and | humid, like the | depth on
    depth of | lustre
Hid i' the | harebell, while her | tresses, sunnier | than
    the wild-grape | cluster,
                        (Mertoun's Song)

Cristina also belongs here. It merely prints the long eight-measure couplets as though they were tetrameters with intermittent rhyme. This emphasizes the medial pause by following it with a new line; but the light stresses trip it into four-four time exactly as in *Home Thoughts, From the Sea, or in Mertoun's Song.*

> She should | never have looked | at me
> If she | meant I should not | love her!
> There are | plenty . . . men, you | call such,
> I sup | pose . . . she may dis | cover
> All her | soul to, if she | pleases,
> And yet | leave much as she | found them
> But I'm | not so, and she | knew it
> When she | fixed me, glancing | round them.
>
> (*Cristina*)

Love Among the Ruins is likely to be felt in time units of four rather than two syllables. This metre has usually been considered trochaic; but the first syllable in each long line is never emphatic and seldom suggests direct attack, while the fifth syllable rarely demands emphasis. When there is a marked difference in the strength of the stress on every other syllable, the trochaic rhythm cannot maintain itself; for the heavy stresses falling upon the third, seventh, and eleventh syllables establish the time as four-four, and the measures as dipodic.

> Where the | quiet-colored | end of evening | smiles   Miles and |
> miles
> On the | solitary | pastures where our | sheep   Half-a | sleep
> Tinkle | homeward through the | twilight, stray or |stop   As
> they| crop—
> Was the | site once of a | city great and | gay,   (So they | say)
> Of our | country's very | capital, its | prince   Ages | since
> Held his | court in, gathered | councils, wielding | far   Peace or |
> war.

This holds equally true for the *Epilogue to Asolando.*

The varying line length and the intermittent rhyme,
however, give a different effect.

At the | midnight in the | silence of the | sleep-time,
      When you | set your fancies | free,
Will they | pass to where—by | death, fools think, im | prisoned—
Low he | lies who once so | loved you, whom you | loved so,
      —Pity | me?

The ballad, *Hervé Riel,* is in four-four time; it differs from the other poems in its diversity of line length and stanza form, and in the frequent use of a rest instead of the fourth syllable in the measure. The rhythm is excellently suited to the rapid movement and stirring nature of the ballad.

I

On the | sea and at the | Hogue, sixteen | hundred ninety- | two,
     Did the | English fight the | French,—woe to | France!
And, the | thirty-first of | May, helter- | skelter through the | blue,
Like a | crowd of frightened | porpoises a | shoal of sharks
          pur | sue,
     Came | crowding ship on | ship to Saint | Malo on the | Rance,
With the | English fleet in | view.

A Woman's Last Word is always approaching four-four time, sometimes actually falling into it, but always checked immediately by the short lines of the stanza; it is, for most readers, I imagine, in duple rhythm.

But the *Epilogue to Fifine at the Fair* permits of no doubt; it reads itself and will hardly be forced into any other rhythm. In contrast to those poems we have already observed, the first syllable of each line of the *Epilogue* demands emphasis and begins with direct attack. The four-four time is very quickly established, and carries on in spite of the many variations in the composition of the measures. These variations are usually in the form of rests in the third measure, often taking the place of two syllables.

| Savage I was | sitting in my ⌐ house, late, | lone:
 | Dreary, | weary with the | long day's | work:
| Head of me, | heart of me, | stupid as a | stone:
 | Tongue-tied | now, now blas | pheming like a | Turk;
| When, in a | moment, just a | knock, call, | cry,
 | Half a pang and | all a rapture, | there again were | we!—
| "What, and is it | really you a | gain?" quoth | I:
 | "I again, what | else did you ex | pect?" quoth | She.

Through The Metidja to Abd-El-Kadr is also in four-four time. It is easy to believe Domett's statement that Browning composed this poem on horseback while riding for his health. The quadruple rhythm perfectly suggests the easy lope of the horse, and the pleasantly monotonous rise and fall of the rider to the time of the hoof-beats.[1] This sensation is conveyed partly by the dipodic swing of the movement (any other movement throws the steed out of gait), and partly by the constant insistence of the monorhyme occurring thirteen times in each eight lines. In five of the lines, a rest fills the time up of an absent syllable after the emphatic internal rhyme; it further emphasizes the sensation of riding.

> As I | ride, as I | ride,
> With a | full heart for my | guide,
> So its | tide rocks my | side,
> As I | ride, as I | ride,
> That, as | I were double- | eyed,
> He, in | whom our Tribes con | fide,
> Is des | cried, ways un | tried,
> As I | ride, as I | ride,

Triple movement, in which the unstressed syllables are felt to be nearer to the preceding accent than to

---

[1] Thomson's attempt to identify this metre with the ionic a majore is interesting, but, like the attempt to find the lesser ionic in *A Pretty Woman*, is forced and unconvincing and, also, we think, unnecessary. His own doubts of his theory persuade him to anticipate those of the reader by claiming for himself at least the bravery of attacking the problem. (*The Rhythm of Speech*, p. 345.)

the following, is a fast galloping measure, fit for *Bringing the Good News from Ghent to Aix*. But in the dipodic measures of *Through the Metidja* the unstressed syllables are associated more closely with the following than with the preceding stressed syllable; it lopes where the other gallops.

The final proof that Browning never regarded versifications as a mere "outward crust" of his thought when he was at his lyric best is the perfection of his metrical art in this poem. The case could be rested on the three lines of each stanza which break the monotonous beat of the rhyme and omit the strong cesura after the rhyme in the first measure. Without this relief, the poem is artistically inconceivable, as the following revision will quickly show:

> As I ride, as I ride,
> With my pride for my guide,
> So its tide rocks my side,
> As I ride, as I ride,
> The homocide, double-eyed,
> In whose tribe, we confide,
> Is described, ways untried,
> As I ride, as I ride.

SELECTED BIBLIOGRAPHY

Andrews, C. E. *The Writing and Reading of Verse*, 1920.

Alden, R. M. *English Verse*, 1903; *An Introduction to Poetry*, 1909.

Bayfield, M. A. *The Measures of the Poets*, 1919.

Beatty, A. *Browning's Verse-form, Its Organic Character*, 1897. (Diss.)

Bleier, Karl. *Die technik Robert Brownings in seinen dramatischen Monologen*, 1901. (Diss.)

Bulkeley, H. J. *The Reasonable Rhythm of Some of Browning's Poems*, London Browning Society Papers, Vol. II.

Corson, Hiram. *A Primer of English Verse*, 1893.

Curry, S. S. *Browning and the Dramatic Monologue*, 1908. (Not Metrical.)

Dabney, Julia P. *The Musical Basis of Verse*, 1901.

Drinkwater, John. *Victorian Poetry*, 1924.

Fogerty, E. *Speaking of English Verse*, 1923.

Goodell, T. D. *Quantity in English Verse, American Philological Association's Transactions*, Vol. XVI. 78-103.

Hodgson, Shadworth. *Outcast Essays and Verse Translations*, 1881.

Klug, Adam. *Untersuchungen über Robert Brownings verskunst*, 1908. (Diss.)

Lewis, C. M. *The Principles of English Verse*, 1906.

Liddell, M. H. *An Introduction to the Scientific Study of English Poetry*, 1902.

Matthews, Brander. *A Study of Versification*, 1911.

Mayor, J. B. *Chapters on English Metre*, 2nd ed., 1901.

Morton, E. P. *The Technique of English non-dramatic Blank Verse*, 1910. (Diss.)

Omond, T. S. *A Study of Metre*, 1903.

Parrott, Thos. M. *Examination of Non-dramatic Poems in Robert Browning's First and Second Periods*, 1893. (Diss.)

Richardson, C. P. *A Study of English Rhyme*, 1909.

Saintsbury, G. E. B. *History of English Prosody*, Vol III, 1910.

Schipper, Jakob. *Englische Metrik* (Vol. 3) 1882; *History of English Versification*, 1910.

Smith, Egerton. *The Principles of English Metre*, 1923.

Thomson, William. *The Rhythm of Speech*, 1923.

Verrier, P. *Essai sur les Principes de la Metrique Anglaise* Vols. I-III, 1909.

INDEX

INDEX

Index to Poems